Furnace of Doubt

Furnace of Doubt

DOSTOEVSKY
&
"The Brothers Karamazov"

Arther Trace

Sherwood Sugden & Company
PUBLISHERS

315 Fifth Street, Peru, Illinois 61354

ACKNOWLEDGEMENTS

All quotations from *The House of the Dead*, *Crime and Punishment*, *The Possessed*, and *The Brothers Karamazov* are from the translations of Constance Garnett.

Quotations from *A Disgraceful Affair* are in the translation by Nora Gottlieb and those from *Notes from the Underground* and *The Dream of a Ridiculous Man* are in the translation of David Magarshack, as they all appear in *Great Short Works of Fyodor Dostoevsky*, ed. Ronald Hingley (New York: Harper and Row, 1968).

Quotations from *The Idiot* are in the translation of David Magarshack (Baltimore, MD: Penguin Books, 1955).

Quotations from "Bobok" are from *Diary of a Writer*, trans. Boris Brasol (New York: Scribner's Sons, 1949. vol. I, pp. 43–57).

The translation of the passage on p. 26 is from Ralph E. Matlaw's edition of *Notes from the Underground and the Grand Inquisitor* Appendix, pp. 21, 194–95 (New York: E. P. Dutton and Co., 1960).

Quotations from *The Raw Youth* are from Andrew McAndrew's translation of *The Adolescent* (as he renders the title) (Garden City, NY: Doubleday and Company, Anchor Books, 1972).

(Quotations from Soviet textbooks, as they appear in Chapter VII, are in my own translation.)

First Edition

Sherwood Sugden & Company, Publishers
315 Fifth Street
Peru, Illinois 61354

Printed and bound in the United States of America.

Library of Congress Cataloging-in-Publication Data

Trace, Arther S.
    Furnace of doubt : Dostoevsky & "The brothers Karamazov" / Arther
Trace.
    179 pp.   cm.
    ISBN 0-89385-030-6 : $8.95
    1. Dostoyevsky, Fyodor, 1821-1881. Brat'ía Karamazovy.
2. Dostoyevsky, Fyodor, 1821-1881--Religion.   I. Title.
PG3325.B73T73 1988
891.73'3--dc19   88-31124
                                                   CIP

TABLE OF CONTENTS

It was not as a child that I learned to believe in Christ and confess his faith. My Hosanna has burst forth from a huge furnace of doubt.
— Fyodor Mikhailovich Dostoevsky, 1880

CHAPTER I

DOSTOEVSKY BEFORE
THE BROTHERS KARAMAZOV

Soon after Dostoevsky published *The Idiot* he indicated a desire to write, as he put it, "some work that
will as far as possible express the whole of what I think."
At the time he had in mind his proposed novel *Atheism*,
which, however, he never wrote. The closest he came to
a work which expressed the whole of what he thought is
The Brothers Karamazov. Compared to the fullness of
The Brothers Karamazov every other work of Dostoevsky's is fragmentary. His other mature novels—*Crime and
Punishment*, *The Idiot*, *The Possessed*, and *The Raw
Youth*—are perhaps best thought of as warm-up exercises for *The Brothers Karamazov*. The artistry of *Crime
and Punishment* may rival that of *The Brothers
Karamazov* but the philosophical depths of that novel,
though far deeper than those of almost anyone else's
novels, are actually Dostoevsky's shallows. There is a sad
falling off in the artistry of *The Idiot*, *The Possessed*, and
especially *The Raw Youth*, even though these novels are
more philosophically sophisticated than *Crime and
Punishment*. None of them can approach the combination of consummate artistry and philosophical penetration
of *The Brothers Karamazov*.

These estimates are not revolutionary, for in recent
years many of those who know Dostoevsky's works

recognize that his achievement in *The Brothers Karamazov* is unmatched by anything else he ever wrote. It
is, above all, the novel one must know if one wants to
know Dostoevsky, and it is out of this realization that I
have undertaken a detailed study of it. I should like,
however, in this chapter to examine briefly the development of Dostoevsky's philosophical and religious thought
as it is revealed in his earlier works in order to suggest
their relationship to *The Brothers Karamazov*.

In some ways life is more nearly an escape from
Dostoevsky than Dostoevsky is an escape from life.
Somehow life itself doesn't commonly confront the
reader so starkly or so agonizingly with the basic questions of human existence as Dostoevsky does. And yet
the questions Dostoevsky raises about the meaning of
human existence—and answers—are the very questions
that must be asked, and answered, not only to get the
maximum meaning from life, but also to make certain
that civilization remains civilized.

In arriving at his own understanding of the meaning
of life Dostoevsky had to confront what is perhaps the
most fundamental and eternal of all philosophical questions, namely: how much decency is natural to the
human heart? Is natural man totally depraved as Calvin
and Hobbes believed? Or is he wholly benevolent in his
nature as Shaftesbury and Rousseau and the most influential intellectuals of the 19th century, and indeed
many of the 20th century, would have us believe? Or is
he morally neuter, being born with no natural inclinations toward either benevolence or malevolence, as
Locke and Helvetius and some contemporary intellectuals believe? Or, again, is he full of both good and bad
instincts which pull him now this way, now that, as

Western civilization has almost universally held until some two hundred years ago? Dostoevsky came to regard the question of the moral nature of man as fundamental. He had to answer it before he could answer any other.

Dostoevsky estimated human nature variously at various times in his life. In his early works, such as *Poor Folk*, *White Nights*, and *Netochka Nezvanova*, he tended toward a sentimental, even naive view of the goodness of human nature without even asking himself where all this goodness came from. At the same time he had no very profound understanding of the evil in man either. But as his art and life progressed, and as he began to write again after his Siberian years, he came more and more to recognize the evil in men's natures, as his *Memoirs from a Deadhouse*, *The Insulted and the Injured*, *Notes from the Underground*, and *Crime and Punishment* suggest, without however losing sight of the goodness that is also in human nature. Indeed as his thought and art and experience further matured he went through what might be called a dark period, his most pessimistic phase, in which the characters in his novels are almost unrelievedly weak, if not downright evil. These include above all *The Idiot*, which (except for Prince Myshkin, who is not of this world) is a relentless study of the vices and follies and crimes of mankind. This period may also be said to include *The Possessed*, and such short works as *Bobok*. Through it all Dostoevsky was expressing a vast compassion for men and women in their fallen condition, except, as we shall see, when they seriously entertain or act upon atheistic principles. *The Raw Youth* and *The Dream of a Ridiculous Man* provide a kind of twilight of optimism again, and finally, with *The Brothers Karamazov*, he returns to an optimistic but vastly fuller and better-balanced understanding of man's nature than he had ever before achieved. In short, in his early works he tended to believe that man is better than he is; in his post-Siberian works he tended to believe that man is worse than he is, until in *The Brothers Kara-mazov* he finally came to an understanding of how good and how bad they really are, that is, that there is good in man, but not nearly enough to enable him to get along without God.

This conclusion is a fundamental premise of Dostoev-sky's dialectic as it appears in *The Brothers Karamazov*, and its significance must therefore be fully understood. As Dostoevsky was gradually concluding that there is so much evil in men's natures that only God can keep them from destroying themselves and one another, most of the intellectuals of his century, and indeed in the preceeding century in Western Europe (only subsequently in Russia itself) were gradually coming to the opposite conclusion, namely, that there is far more good in men's natures than Christianity had taught—so much good, in fact, that religion is not needed after all, and that there may not be a God in any case.

The mature Dostoevsky came to recognize that the influence of the Enlighteners' unbounded faith in the natural goodness of natural man was reaching crisis pro-portions, and he perceived that therefore the new faith in unaided reason and in science and the simultaneous loss of religious faith would in time lead to Russia's ruin. By 1870 he saw his role as one of reminding his countrymen that the Christian view of man was the right view, indeed the only view that could save Russia, and that the Enlighteners' view—and the view of the Russian radicals —would in time destroy Russia, to say nothing of civ-ilization itself.

Dostoevsky had not, however, always had this fear of the rationalist-socialist-intellectual establishment. In fact he was part of it during the brief years that he was under the spell of Belinsky's ardent rhetoric and of the utopian dreamers of the Petrashevsky Circle. At the same time, however, he was studying human nature in his own private way, and what most attracted his attention was the problem of suffering and the psychology of suffering, not physical suffering so much as moral and emotional suffering, suffering that comes especially from feelings of loneliness and inferiority and guilt.

The professional sufferers of Dostoevsky's early stories are usually good people, poor and lonely, but good, even sentimentally good. It was only later, as he moved toward religious belief, that he was able to make sense out of suffering. In the meantime he was content merely to acknowledge it and to depict it. His pre-Siberian stories deal primarily with losers, and there is no loser like a Dostoevsky loser. No one is more miserable or more pathetic. In reading *Poor Folk* one experiences the supreme agony of Makar Devushkin in his hopeless love for the hapless Varvara. Golyadkin, in *The Double*, is a double loser. Polzunkov in the story of that name rends the reader's heart as he makes a fool of himself in order to amuse other people, and then, in his painfully pathetic way, tries to get them to respect him too. Ordinov too, and Katerina in *The Landlady* are typical Dostoevsky losers.

Even Dostoevsky's winners are losers. The tortured soul of the unnamed hero of *White Nights* is so badly off that in his loneliness he celebrates the anniversaries of his happy dreams, and when he experiences three days of real-life love he is so grateful that, even after Nastenka runs off with his rival, he concludes that these three days of love are worth a lifetime of dreams. And Vasya Shumkin, in *A Faint Heart*, is, in his bad luck, so overwhelmed by a minor stroke of good luck that his mind snaps, out of sheer gratitude.

The hostile and sadistic forces in human nature had not yet come very far within Dostoevsky's artistic ken. The characters in *Poor Folk* and *White Nights*, it is true, are capable of torturing one another, but they do so inadvertently, and out of love, not hate. Even characters like the violinist Efimov in *Netochka Nezvanova* and Yermalyan in *The Honest Thief* are depicted not as evil, really, but merely as weak and hence pathetic, more nearly victims of evil than agents of it. Even the sexual precocity of Netochka herself, and of *The Little Hero*, seem innocent enough; and Mr. Prokharchin, in the work of that name, is more pitiable perhaps than any other miser in literature. There is, it is true, a hint of things to come in *A Christmas Tree and a Wedding*, in the character of Julian Mastakovich, who, along with Bykov in *Poor Folk*, begins a string of Dostoevsky characters in the dirty-old-man tradition.

And yet it would be a mistake to think of Dostoevsky's losers as totally victims of their environment, or of their circumstances, such as Karamzin's *Poor Liza*, for example, or the other sentimental 18th- or 19th-century heroes and heroines who become the victims of others' dark designs. Dostoevsky's losers are losers primarily because they are their own worst enemies. They suffer from masochistic impulses which often come from feelings of isolation or guilt. They revel in their misery; they are capable of seeking out misery in a way that is beyond the capacities of the Byronic and Germanic heroes, or the "superfluous man" tradition of

Russian literature. It is this propensity for self-destruction that does most to distinguish Dostoevsky's early characters from the characters of fiction before and during his time.

In general, then, the reader is overwhelmed by the goodness of human nature represented in Dostoevsky's early stories, stories of dreamers, meek types, self-destructive, but still meek and dreamy. It seems a bit ironic to conclude that in these stories Dostoevsky was still naive about human nature, because even in these he showed more understanding of the human psyche than most writers (including many great writers, even in their mature works). Dostoevsky was naive about human nature in these stories only if we consider them against the vastly greater understanding of human nature which the further development of his life and art was to afford. In these early works Dostoevsky had hardly dipped his toe into the cesspool of man's depravity. After his years in prison, however, he was ready to take the plunge.

In their meekness and goodness, most of the characters in Dostoevsky's early stories would not even squash a lady-bug. During his four-year incarceration in the prison at Omsk, Dostoevsky met convicts who squashed ladies; one convict even chopped up little children. Furthermore, they did so with no remorse, and would squash and chop again if given the opportunity. There can be no question that Dostoevsky's estimate of human nature underwent a transformation as a result of his prison experience. He came to realize that his early stories were based upon an illusion about how good human nature is. There are indeed meek types in the world, and he continued to present meek types in his post-Siberian stories, but he now recognized that human nature is far more rapacious, hostile, vengeful, cruel, destructive, greedy, jealous, lustful, and perverse than he had previously supposed.

Some readers of *Memoirs from a Deadhouse* pounce upon the passages illustrating Dostoevsky's faith in "the golden heart," which occasionally appear in the narrative, especially descriptions of such timid criminal types as the young Tartar, Aley, who was the soul of goodness and "chaste as a young maiden," Sirotkin, who was "neat, gentle, pensive," and the kind-hearted and selfless Sushilov, all of whom seem to suggest that Dostoevsky had succeeded in finding much good among his fellow convicts. Indeed Dostoevsky observed in a letter to his brother Michael a week after he was released, that "in four years in prison I came at least to distinguish human beings from criminals. Believe me, there are deep, strong, beautiful characters among them, and what a joy it was to discover the good beneath the coarse hard surface. And not one, not two, but several." But several is still not many, and the dominant impression of the *Memoirs* cannot overall be said to redound to the glory of the human race. As Goryanichikov, Dostoevsky's autobiographical hero, says, "Speaking generally, I may say that, with the exception of a few indefatigably cheerful fellows who were consequently regarded with contempt by everyone, they were all sullen, envious, dreadfully vain, boastful people. . . . The majority of them were corrupt and horribly depraved."

Significantly, the political prisioners, of whom Dostoevsky himself was one, interested him less than the ferocious felons, the cold-blooded murderers and the professional sadists, whose deeds and minds are duly described. He was awed by the fact that men are capable of vastly dirtier deeds than he had ever before imagined, and he was awed by nothing so much as the unrepentance of the unrepentant criminal. "Surely it would have been possible," his autobiographical hero observes, "during all those years to have noticed, to have detected something, to have caught some glimpse which would have borne witness to some inner anguish and suffering in those hearts. But it was not there, it certainly was not there." Ultimately what Dostoevsky learned from his prison experience was, not that those who are in prison are much worse than those who are out of prison, but that those out of prison are not all that much better than those in prison.

As a result of this experience, Dostoevsky never again allowed himself to be deluded into believing that human nature is as good as the European Enlighteners, the German Romantics—including his beloved Schiller—and his Russian revolutionary ex-friends said that it was; he never again let himself dream of the humanitarian utopias of leading intellectuals, either in Western Europe or in Russia itself. He began to recognize how unutterably false, indeed how dangerous, were the premises and promises of Belinsky and the Fourierist members of the Petrashevsky Circle who had influenced his youthful years. If he were to come to the truth about life, then he would have to accommodate his thinking to a vastly more realistic estimate of human nature than he had done heretofore. It was still to be some time, however, before he addressed himself seriously to the question which later most occupied him, namely, if man is by nature so inclined to evil, then how can civilization be preserved? And how can it be preserved without sacrificing man's dignity? He had still not demonstrated either to himself or to anyone else that religion was the only possible answer.

In *The Insulted and the Injured*, which was written about the same time as *Memoirs from a Deadhouse*, and which had grander artistic pretensions, Dostoevsky shows a much broader understanding of the wickedness in human nature than is evident in his pre-Siberian stories. Prince Volkhovsky is the first of Dostoevsky's fully developed characters whom one can genuinely hate in good conscience. The things he has done, or says he has done, cause a stench to rise from the page unequalled by the doings of any of Dostoevsky's pre-Siberian characters. He not only ruins the lives of most of the characters in the novel, but tells us how he ruined the lives, in the nastiest, most disgusting ways, of characters that are *not* in the novel. Clearly, Dostoevsky will not henceforth be hoodwinked by the sentimental vaporings of intellectuals carrying on about the natural goodness of man (despite his own occasional sallies into sentimentality not only in this work but in works that were to come).

He proceeded to launch a kind of one-man crusade to put the radical intellectuals of the West on notice that man in his natural condition was not nearly so kind and reasonable as they said he was, and that no amount of social engineering would fill the land with utopian goodness. Some of Dostoevsky's works seem to be aimed specifically at correcting the Enlighteners' view of the nature of man and so to prepare the ground for a study of natural man as he is represented in *The Brothers Karamazov*. I should like therefore to examine them briefly.

Dostoevsky had suggested in *A Disgraceful Affair* (1862) that there is not enough goodness in human nature to bring about moral reform on the basis of merely humanitarian ideals. Ivan Ilych, the theoretical humanitarian, in his efforts to administer a "moral embrace" to one of his lowly employees on his wedding day, interrupts the festivities with a lecture on moral aims and ideals, which leads to the guests' intense distaste for him

and his for them. He generously samples the bridegroom's liquor, and, on discovering that he has a talent
for spitting, directs "a huge gob of spittle" into the face of
one of the guests. He then sinks back into his chair in a
drunken stupor before dropping his head into a plate of
blancmange. A few moments later he staggers away from
the table, falls flat on the floor, and passes out. His
respectful hosts, thereupon, yield up to him their bridal
bed and they themselves substitute for it a mattress and
some chairs. Unfortunately, under the vigor of a physical
embrace the makeshift bed collapses in the night, bring-
ing shrieks from the bride, and raising the whole
household. The bride's mother gets so angry with the
bridegroom for tolerating such a boor that she leads her
daughter away, leaving him to spend the rest of the night
alone. When Ivan Ilych regains his senses, he experiences
a fit of genuine remorse which lasts eight days, during
which time he even entertains the notion of joining a
monastery, with tonsure and all. At the end of the story,
we see him looking at himself in the mirror and exclaiming, "I have failed to live up to my ideals."

It turns out that the real hero of the story, or rather
the truth-bearer, is Ivan Ilych's friend, Stepan Niko-
forovich. Stepan in his wisdom has accurately taken the
moral measure of natural man and warns Ivan beforehand that man is not good enough to live up to his merely
humanitarian ideals. And Dostoevsky's story would have
us believe that indeed he is not.

But such ideals are not merely the invention of Russian officials like Ivan Ilych. They are also the ideals of
Russian intellectuals such as Chernyshevsky, Dobrolyubov, Herzen, and others, and they are not far
removed from the ideals of the Western European
Enlighteners of the previous century, from whom Rus-

sian radical thought ultimately derived. Ivan Ilych is
merely one of a string of Dostoevsky's unreformed
reformers who culminate in Rakitin in *The Brothers
Karamazov.*

A Disgraceful Affair is thus good preparation for
Notes from the Underground in which Dostoevsky again
attacks the Enlighteners' rosy view of rational man, but
this time he does so much more powerfully. *Notes from
the Underground* is above all a polemic; it simply happens to be a powerful and highly artistic polemic by a
powerfully artistic writer. It constitutes a devastating attack not merely upon Chernyshevsky's socialist utopia
symbolized by the tidy Crystal Palace created for the
1852 London Exposition, but upon the whole passel of
rationalist philosophers of Enlightened Europe—both
West and East—and their disciples. What Dostoevsky is
attacking in *Notes from the Underground* is not so much
the Enlighteners' naive faith in human reason as their
naive faith in human nature, upon which their whole
philosophical edifice was constructed. It was their
massive miscalculation of the true nature of man that
Dostoevsky insisted was leading them and the world
astray. Man is not only not very rational; he is downright
perverse, and it was the fact that man could, would, and
should stick out his tongue at the Crystal Palace that the
Enlighteners and the socialist and scientific utopians had
failed to take into account. Dostoevsky is telling us that
Perverseness is man's middle name. It is the best evidence
of his free will, of his humanness, and it is what makes
the Underground Man more "alive," as he himself says,
than the rest of us.

By the time Dostoevsky published *Notes from the
Underground* he not only was no longer naive about

human nature but he had become acutely aware of man's spite, his sado-masochistic impulses, his pleasure not only in pain but in despair and degradation, his base desires, his malice, his inclination to revel in the most revolting acts, and his inclination to be contemptuous not only of others, but of himself. We find the Underground Man exercising his perverseness even on page one, where he tells us that he refuses out of spite to see a doctor for a cure for his diseased liver, and by the time the story ends he is still exercising it by performing a charitable act, namely reforming the prostitute Liza, out of sheer sadistic perverseness.

Nor are we to take the Underground Man himself as a mere freak of human nature in the exercise of his perverse capacities. On the contrary, the Underground Man is Everyman, or perhaps more accurately, a personification of the perverseness in Everyman, an exaggerated perverseness to be sure, but exaggerated to demonstrate that perverseness is so bald a fact of human nature that, as the Underground Man says, "it sets at naught all our classifications and shatters all the systems set up by the lovers of the human race for the happiness of the human race."

Similarly *The Idiot* is best read not merely as the story of "a wholly beautiful man," to use Dostoevsky's own words, but also as a reaffirmation of the natural badness of man by exposing some choice specimens of men and women to the company of this truly good man so that we may watch the chemical reaction and examine the residue. The chief thing to understand about Prince Myshkin is not merely that he is untainted by sin, but that he is untaintable. He is prelapsarian man, and he cannot be corrupted. He is an ideal, he is No Man, or if not No

Man then a man from another planet. Indeed, in his notebooks on *The Idiot* Dostoevsky wrote in large letters, "N.B. The Prince *is* Christ."

But St. Petersburg society being what it is, i.e., like the rest of humankind, it is no wonder that by the end of the novel Prince Myshkin in all his incorruptible innocence has not only witnessed but sometimes inadvertently contributed to Ganya's greed and envy, General Ivolgin's lying and drunkenness, Aglaya's cruelty, Lebedev's hypocrisy, Natasha's hatred and slander and jealousy, Ippolit's spite, Totsky's sensuality, and a whole host of other sins, large and small, almost the whole gamut of unoriginal sins, topped off by Rogozhin's lust for, and finally murder of, Natasha. So that Myshkin in the end reacts as only a pure soul could react after experiencing these adventures "among people." He cannot be destroyed by them, because Dostoevsky has a more powerful way of conveying the horror of human behavior than letting Rogozhin murder him, which is why his epileptic fit saves his life just as Rogozhin comes at him with his favorite knife. No, Myshkin reacts to contact with people of this world by lapsing back into the idiocy which he suffered in a sanatorium in Switzerland before he was cured and came into the real world. It is a powerful ending and a powerful commentary on human nature that a truly good man cannot endure the evils of the world and still maintain his sanity. As Dostoevsky's mentor, Honoré de Balzac, observed, "A good man can't remain long in this world." The Prince is everywhere surrounded by selfishness and he in his pure selflessness has no chance. Indeed, in a sinful world a truly good man seems like a sick man. As Princess Belkonsky says of him, "You can see for yourself the sort of man he is—a sick man."

And yet it is not that the people Prince Myshkin encounters are personifications of unmitigated evil. They are not, and in fact Myshkin feels sorry for them all, even Rogozhin after he has killed Natasha, whom the Prince loved with all his bodiless spirit; for in the catastrophic climax he is comforting him just as he would comfort any other human being. Some of the earthlings in *The Idiot* are even good-hearted and generous, for all their exhibitions of selfishness and passion. Some are capable of feeling great guilt and hence great suffering, which underscores their humanness as opposed to their beastliness, and indeed we are ourselves invited to feel sorry for them all, though in our weakness we cannot help feeling less sorry for some than for others.

Thus Dostoevsky in still another way answers those intellectuals of both Western Europe and Russia itself who would have us believe that all men are immaculately conceived, by putting all men up against a man who is truly immaculately conceived, so that we may not delude ourselves as the rationalist and scientific intellectuals of 19th-century Europe were deluding both themselves and millions upon millions of others. The more Prince Myshkin's friends ridicule him and call him an idiot and a fool the more they confirm their own fallen nature. Like most of the characters in the novel, the reader, if he is not careful, finds himself totalling up Prince Myshkin's failures rather than his own, and so misses the whole point of the novel.

The Idiot is very nearly the most profoundly pessimistic work that Dostoevsky ever wrote. But there is one that is even more pessimistic, more shudderingly pessimistic, despite its humor, namely *Bobok*. In this little story Dostoevsky again hits hard and tellingly at his contemporaries' misevaluation of man's natural goodness, this time by presenting to us a picture of human nature in the next world. Here the narrator sits down in a graveyard and before long begins to hear voices of the inhabitants of the graves around him. They come from a general, a "prominent lady," a bureaucrat, an engineer, a baron, a shopkeeper, and a 16-year-old giggling girl, in short, from a fair cross-section of human society. They are all aware that they are dead, but they still retain a "consciousness," a reprieve, so to speak, of two or three months in order to repent their sins and prepare themselves for eternity. Their bodies give off a putrid odor which they understand to be a "moral stench." But how do they spend these precious days? They play cards, they quarrel, one tries to collect a debt from another, they aim at a state in which they feel ashamed of nothing and hence try to enjoy these days free from conscience and moral responsibility, they long to appear nude before each other, and they practice mental lechery. At length, the narrator sneezes and the noise causes an immediate "sepulchral silence" to come over the graveyard. Then the narrator exclaims, "Depravity in such a place; debauch of ultimate hopes, debauch of flabby and rotting corpses—even without sparing the last moments of consciousness! They're given—given gratuitously—these moments, and. . . . But the main, the cardinal point is— in a place such as this! No, this I can't concede . . . I'll try other graves. I'll listen everywhere. That's really the thing to do; I must listen everywhere, and not merely in some one spot, in order to form a judgment. Perhaps I'll also strike something comforting."

But the narrator knows, as Dostoevsky knows, that human nature is pretty much the same all over, and that there are few people who will use these precious two months to prepare their souls before all life is taken from them and their last words become a babbling bit of nonsense, "Bobok, Bobok," which means that the end of their reprieve is near and that Judgment Day is imminent.

Bobok is a harsh exposé of man's moral culpability, without so much as a hint of sympathy for men as fallen creatures. Dostoevsky's final position on human nature is that men are indeed fallen creatures; but in view of what they were before the Fall, and in view of their vast moral and spiritual capacities even after the Fall, they still deserve all the compassion they can get, however horribly their instincts and passions lead them astray. This position was already well defined in *The Idiot*, which was written some five years before *Bobok*, and in which Dostoevsky's perspective and understanding of human nature was already so broad that he invites the reader, insofar as the reader is able, to judge human nature through the eyes of the ideally good man, Prince Myshkin, who in his goodness is the soul of compassion, even for Rogozhin as murderer.

The theme of compassion for fallen man comes through again in *The Dream of a Ridiculous Man*, which in a sense is the story of *The Idiot* in reverse. In *The Idiot*, Dostoevsky shows us the behavior of a society of fallen people in the presence of an incorruptible hero who is, figuratively speaking, from another planet. In *The Dream of a Ridiculous Man* he shows us the behavior of a society of uncorrupted people in the presence of a fallen hero who is literally from another planet.

In his dream, the Ridiculous Man, an earthling, is spirited off to a planet in another solar system by some dark mysterious creature, a planet just like the earth except that this planet is "untainted by the Fall, inhabited by people who had not sinned and who lived in the same paradise as that in which . . . our parents lived before they sinned." The Ridiculous Man is dazzled by the goodness and beauty of these people, whom he sees as just like the people on earth would have been had there been no Fall. He can't understand them very well because he is himself fallen—just as the people in St. Petersburg society cannot understand Prince Myshkin very well. But, like Adam and Eve, corrupted by Satan, so these beautiful people are corrupted by their fallen visitor. "Like the germ of a plague infecting whole kingdoms," he says, "I corrupted them all." And in their corruption they begin to act like the fallen creatures on earth. They invent morality because now there was immorality; they make a virtue of shame, whereas before they had no need for shame; they invent the concept of honor because now there is such a thing as dishonor; they invent justice because now there is injustice; and they invent brotherhood and friendship because there is hatred. Saints appear because so many people are no longer saints. They even cease to believe that they once existed in an uncorrupt condition and dismiss such thoughts as fairy tales.

Moreover, their culture and ideals begin to look more and more like those of 19th-century Europe. They begin to put their faith in science as the source of all wisdom and the key to happiness. Social engineers appear who propose plans which, even though they impinge upon their freedom, and indeed their dignity, were designed to produce a "harmonious society"; and they propose to exterminate those who will not work toward a harmonious society. Tyrants arise and, in their search for power, advocate crimes. Suffering begins to appear on their faces, and the more they live the more they suffer, and they make suffering a virtue. As the Ridiculous Man watches them in their struggle and their suffering he comes to love them more than he did before their fall. "I loved the earth they had polluted even more than when it had been a paradise, and only because sorrow had made its appearance on it," he exclaims.

When he awakes from his dream, the Ridiculous Man is overcome by "rapture, infinite and boundless rapture," and he resolves as long as he lives to preach the truth about the dream revealed to him, the truth that "the main thing is love your neighbor as yourself," so that people can be happy without losing their ability to love on earth, "even if there never is a heaven on earth." And so in his new perspective the Ridiculous Man sees that fallen men deserve all the sympathy they can get. The overwhelming despair which, before his dream, had led him to resolve upon suicide, was now replaced not only with the intense desire to go on living but to love and help others. Dostoevsky, too, by this time had seen the truth, and indeed he himself was to go on preaching the truth as long as he lived: the truth about man's fallen nature and about his divine nature.

It may seem incredible that Dostoevsky should have to belabor the point about man's corrupt nature time and time again, even in his best works, for it had been the view of most of the centuries of the civilized world, and the view of virtually all the great religions, including Christianity, as well as the view of common experience. But it had not been the view of the 18th-century Enlighteners, and it was not the view of the 19th-century romantics and radicals, and it was their thinking that was in the saddle and was riding mankind — riding it, in Dostoevsky's view, to the end of civilization.

But if men are not any better than they are by nature, then what is going to make them good enough to keep civilization civilized? This question perpetually plagued Dostoevsky after his Siberian years, and his ultimate conclusion was that only religion could save men from

themselves and hence save civilization. "How is man going to be good without God?" Dimitri Karamazov ex-
claimed; "I always keep coming back to that question."
Dostoevsky also kept coming back to that question, and
some years before he wrote *The Brothers Karamazov* he
had already concluded that the question was rhetorical.
In Dostoevsky's view the 19th-century romantics and
radicals, both in Russia and in Western Europe, for all
their admirable pleas for humanity and the rights of man,
did not perceive that ultimately the preservation of
humanity and human rights depended squarely upon the
preservation of religion, which in turn ultimately depended upon the Church, which in turn depended upon the
authority of Sacred Scripture. And so in seeking to in-
crease man's dignity, they were in effect helping to
destroy it. This was the threat which Dostoevsky sought
to forestall. And his crusade against what he might have
called the Endarkenment began with *Notes from the
Underground*.

There is nothing specifically religious about *Notes
from the Underground* in the form that we have it, even
though it is commonly regarded, and with at least some
justification, as the prelude to Dostoevsky's great novels.
It may well be, however, that the single most important
fact necessary for an understanding of the complexities of
Notes from the Underground, indeed the key to the
meaning of it, is in Dostoevsky's account of a passage
that was omitted from it when it was first published.
That passage signified the increasing role that religion
was playing in his thought. Dostoevsky's account of the
crucial omission appears in a letter to his brother
Michael, dated March 26, 1864, just after *Notes from
the Underground* was published:

> I am bewailing the first part of my *Notes*. Terrible
> misprints, and it would have been better not to reprint the

penultimate chapter at all—that chapter where the very idea is stated [i.e., Chapter X of Part I] than to print it in that form, that is, with sentences left out and contradicting myself. But what is to be done? Those swinish censors left in the passages where I railed at everything and pretended to blaspheme: but they deleted the passages where I deduced from all this *the necessity of faith and Christ* [emphasis Dostoevsky's]. What are they doing, those censors? Are they in league against the government or something?

Although responsible editors of *Notes from the Underground* call attention to the omitted passage referred to in the letter, virtually no Dostoevsky scholar has attempted to account for the passage or to interpret *Notes from the Underground* in the light of it. But if one does examine the *Notes* in the light of the omission as Dostoevsky describes it, the work turns out to mean something rather different from the way it is commonly interpreted. Some may be inclined to say: This is all very well, but in the version we have the passage is after all not there and thus the work must be understood as we have it, not as Dostoevsky says it was meant to be. Furthermore, one may insist, we do not know what the passage was, and it would be dangerous to interpret a work on the basis of a non-existent passage, regardless of what the author says. And it might also be pointed out that when *Notes from the Underground* was reprinted during Dostoevsky's lifetime, he did not add the deleted passage.

And yet there is no doubt that Dostoevsky said what he said, that he said it in the chapter "where the very idea" of *Notes from the Underground* is stated, and that he had "deduced from *all this*, (emphasis mine) "*the necessity of faith and Christ*" (emphasis Dostoevsky's). The remarks are so important because they suggest that the real purpose of *Notes from the Underground* was specifically to demonstrate "*the necessity of faith and*

Christ." We do not know precisely to what he was referring in the words "all this." It could have been only the ideas in Chapter X of Part I, but it seems more likely that he was referring to the whole argument of Part I up to the point of the deleted passage. One may note, too, that Chapter X is a bit short. It seems logical to conjecture that the censored passage originally appeared after the words, "Why have I been provided with all these desires? Was it only to reach the conclusion that they're nothing but a big swindle? Is that the goal of everything? I don't believe it."

How then would Dostoevsky have deduced "from all this the *necessity of faith and Christ*"? By the time he wrote *Notes from the Underground* he had evidently already concluded that if there is no God, then men are no more sinners than the beasts, that they are at best superbeasts. In fact, it turns out that if there is no God-and-immortality then men are worse than the beasts because all the moral suffering of men which stems from illogical sacrifices, from the senseless pursuit of virtue, from an unbeastlike check upon desire, in short from the exercise of free will, constitutes a swindle, what indeed might be called a Cosmic Swindle. In a Godless universe men are even less dignified than the beasts; for God-and-immortality provide the only explanation that can place a value upon the moral suffering that inevitably comes with the exercise of free will. If, when a man dies, the burdocks grow over his grave and that is the end of him, just as it is the end of any dog or frog, then men ought to envy with every ounce of their being the beasts who are not meaninglessly tormented by the terrible burden of free will; for such beasts are good beasts, whereas men are bad beasts. But being beasts nonetheless, the only logical ethic for the beast-man is a beast ethic, and "virtuous men" are men who are acting like fools. The more unbelievers insist upon man's free will and his capacity to suffer therefrom, and the more they insist upon virtue without God-and-immortality, the more they prove that man's free will is indeed a mockery, a swindle, a Cosmic Swindle.

In such a context, then, what is the meaning of desire, as the Underground Man asks? Do man's desires constitute a mockery, a swindle? Do they suffer and die and are buried and do not rise again? "Is that the goal of everything?" the Underground Man asks, and answers, "I don't believe it." In *The Brothers Karamazov* Dostoevsky demonstrates with devastating logic that if man's terrible burden of free will is not to be a swindle, then the only way out is belief in God-and-immortality. It must have been in some such context as this that in *Notes from the Underground* Dostoevsky "deduced from all this" the "necessity of faith and Christ."

The cornerstone of Dostoevsky's entire dialectic is his insistence that man has an immortal soul. "The immortality of the soul," he says in *The Diary of a Writer*, is "the loftiest idea of human existence. Neither a man nor a nation can live without a 'higher idea,' and there is only one such idea on earth, that of an immortal human soul; all the other 'higher ideas' by which men live flow from that."

Dostoevsky understood what many of his fellow intellectuals did not understand, namely that there is no practical value in believing in God without believing in immortality, that indeed God-and-immortality are inseparable; it is either belief in God-and-immortality or belief in no God at all. Many 18th- and 19th-century intellectuals separated God from immortality, and dis-

pensed with immortality whenever they did not also
dispense with God. But Dostoevsky argued that no such
severance can take place. "God *is* immortality," he tells
us over and over again. There is only the merest technical
difference, he would argue, between the deists' belief in
God as the Great Winder-upper and belief in no God at
all. The only God who can have any lasting effect upon
human behavior is a personal God, a God to whom one
can pray, a God who promises immortality, a God who
rewards and punishes in the next life. (The idea that God
rewards and punishes in this life without reference to the
next is contradicted daily by the evidence. Widespread
belief in such a God could not long endure.)

But clearly it is not enough for men to invent immortality on the grounds that men desire it or cannot live
without it, for it is just as easy to reason the doctrine of
immortality out of existence as it is into existence. Even
Voltaire, the great reasoner, recognized the limitations of
reason on this point: "Human reason," he confessed," is
so little able, merely by its own strength, to demonstrate
the immortality of the soul that it was absolutely
necessary that religion should reveal it to us. It is of advantage to society in general that mankind should believe
the soul to be immortal; faith commands us to this."

Having recognized the utter inability of mere reason
or science to solve the truly crucial questions of human
existence, Dostoevsky thus ultimately rests his case with
revelation, with Sacred Scripture, which he recognized as
the only source of truth that can sustain the concept of
personal immortality. As we shall see, in the crucial
places in *The Brothers Karamazov* which deal with the
problem of immortality, Dostoevsky quotes not the
philosophers but the Scriptures.

Beginning with *Crime and Punishment*, Dostoevsky
more and more identified goodness with belief and

badness with unbelief. A brief sampling of the characters in the mature novels will illustrate the phenomenon. Generally speaking the believers are intended as the truth-bearers, and the truth they bear comes from revelation, not from reason or science. They include, for example, Sonya in *Crime and Punishment*, Prince Myshkin in *The Idiot*, Makar Dolgoruky in *The Raw Youth*, Bishop Tikhon in *The Possessed*, and Alyosha and Father Zossima in *The Brothers Karamazov*.

The least sympathetic characters are the professional unbelievers, like Pyotr Verhovensky in *The Possessed* and Rakitin in *The Brothers Karamazov* and diletantish unbelievers like Luzhin and Old Karamazov. There are also the uncomfortable unbelievers who end up as suicides, such as Svidrigailov, Stavrogin, and Smerdyakov. There is also a host of other characters who suffer from varying degrees of unbelief and who may either attempt suicide like Ippolit in *The Idiot* or achieve it on the basis of some theory like Kirillov in *The Possessed* and Kraft in *The Raw Youth*. Another group of characters undergo a spiritual conversion which leads them—or will lead them—to a more or less true religious faith, which meant for Dostoevsky the greatest of all human triumphs. Such characters include Raskolnikov, Old Verhovensky, Shatov, and Ivan Karamazov. These are usually Dostoevsky's most sympathetic characters on account of the agonizing spiritual suffering they endure in becoming believers. By and large the characters in whom Dostoevsky himself was most interested are those who, like himself, came to be believers after having passed through "the furnace of doubt," as Dostoevsky expressed it.

The matter of belief and unbelief becomes so far the informing principle in the mature novels that it overrides all other philosophical considerations, even in *Crime and*

Punishment, which is the story of a good man who starts out with a bad idea, indeed, in Dostoevsky's view the worst idea, the atheistic idea, and ends up, again in Dostoevsky's view, with the best idea, the idea of salvation through Christ.

It is crucial to recognize that Raskolnikov's division of all mankind into two sorts, the ordinary and the extraordinary, is an atheistic idea. He theorizes that the "extraordinary men" have the right to determine for themselves whether ordinary men have any dignity, any worth or not, and hence whether they should or should not be exterminated. For all the mixed motives that account for Raskolnikov's murdering the old pawnbroker, we are to understand that without the impetus of his attempt to demonstrate to himself that he is an extraordinary person and that the pawnbroker is not, he would not have killed her. He imputes to himself the "inner right to step over certain obstacles" to fulfill his idea. He—or rather Dostoevsky—chooses as victim one of the lowest, apparently most "worthless" members of human society, one whose removal therefrom, Raskolnikov eloquently argues, would be no loss to society, but a great gain. Similarly "worthless" characters, it may be noted, are murdered in Dostoevsky's other murder novels in order to make the same point, as Lebyadkin in *The Possessed* and Old Karamazov in *The Brothers Karamazov*, barnacles all on the hull of humanity, and the thing to do with barnacles is to scrape them off. But it turns out that they are not barnacles but human beings like every other human being, complete with immortal souls. Sonya knows that man's worth is therefore to be determined by God and not arbitrarily by men. "Who has made me a judge to decide who is to live and who is not to live?" she declares. This is also what Raskolnikov eventually learns after plowing through an ocean of agony.

Dostoevsky's emphasis upon the sacredness of human life rests squarely upon his recognition that men are not merely fellow creatures, but God's creatures, and that murder breaks not only man's law, which is changeable, but God's law, which is not. And as Dostoevsky also recognizes, this conclusion does not come from reason but from revelation. If mere reason tells us that the worth of a man's life is imputed to him by other men, then reason also tells us that other men can also deny the worth of a man's life, so that human lives can be quite as reasonably exterminated thousands by thousands by a Napoleon as one by one by Raskolnikov. As Porfiry says to Raskolnikov, "If you'd invented another theory you might have done something a thousand times more hideous."

The main point about Raskolnikov's confession is that he does not have to confess. When he learns of Svidrigailov's suicide, he knows that the last barrier to his safety had been removed, for the other characters who know he is the murderer, namely Sonya and Dounia, won't tell. For what does it mean to confess when there is no earthly reason to confess? Raskolnikov's confession becomes an act of faith, faith that there is God-and-immortality, after all, that Christ is a savior, that He has mercy, as Sonya insisted, and that Raskolnikov is therefore doing the right thing by confessing out of recognition that his crime is registered in God's book despite the absence of palpable fact in Porfiry's book.

Thus what Raskolnikov learns is that the truth is not in his head but in Sonya's Bible. And so the novel ends with Dostoevsky's observation that the story of Raskolnikov's "gradual regeneration," of his "passing from one world into another," of his "initiation into a new unknown life," is another story. It is not until the last page of the Epilogue that Raskolnikov in prison picks up Sonya's Bible and begins to read it. If Raskolnikov had not turned to God in the end, then all of his guilt feelings and suffering and confession would have made no sense at all. Indeed the novel would make no sense at all. The Epilogue, philosophically, thus makes the novel, or perhaps even saves the novel.

Dostoevsky intended *The Possessed* to be a cornucopia of the fruits of faithlessness, including suicide, murder, and all manner of brutality and moral ugliness. In fact no other of Dostoevsky's mature novels is so topheavy with unbelievers as *The Possessed*. Among the few believers is Father Tikhon in a suppressed chapter, and even he confesses to Stavrogin that his belief is "imperfect." There is also Shatov, the reformed atheist who merely says that he "will believe," and much of what he does believe did not get transferred from Dostoevsky's notebooks on *The Possessed* to *The Possessed* itself. Actually the burden of belief is borne most notably by Old Verhovensky himself, whose conversion on his death-bed to the teachings of Christianity offers a badly needed note of hope, though its importance is not generally recognized among Dostoevsky scholars.

Clearly, Dostoevsky was far more interested in demonstrating in *The Possessed* the destructive power of atheism than the healing power of religion. In *The Possessed*, more than in any other work outside his *Diary of a Writer*, he wanted to demonstrate the political consequences of atheism, though he by no means neglected personal consequences of atheism, as the fates of such characters as Kirillov and Stavrogin indicate.

By the time Dostoevsky wrote *The Possessed* he had come to realize that the apparently harmless theorizing of "socialist" revolutionaries could readily lead to the kind of revolution that ended in chaos and destruction. He firmly believed, as he said in his *Diary of a Writer*, that the Petrashevists could easily lead to the Nechaivists, that the theorizers about revolution could lead to revolution, and based upon atheistic principles massive bloodshed not only could follow but, on such principles, could *justifiably* follow. Old Verhovensky's "socialist" teachings could lead to Pyotr Verhovensky's outrages. But there is in fact a whole spectrum of unbelief in the novel, for it is a veritable encyclopedia of atheism.

Pyotr Verhovensky is one of Dostoevsky's great logical atheists. He is certain that there is no God, and that therefore, as Ivan Karamazov was to observe, "there is no virtue and everything is lawful." Pyotr aims at the cardinal virtue of the logical unbeliever living in a believing world, namely cleverness, the virtue of pursuing one's own objectives without ending up in prison or being otherwise inconvenienced. As a logical atheist he demonstrates a proper contempt for the poor floundering socialist idealists like his own father, and his co-conspirators, such as Shigalov, Virginsky, Leputin, Lyamshin, Tolkatchenko, and Erkel. All of them in their various ways and their varying degrees of unbelief assume that man can find happiness without God by reconstructing society in accordance with one or another of their utopian plans. Pyotr knows better because he has no illusions about human nature. He has learned from Stavrogin that if there is no God then the world is a jungle, and only a jungle ethic makes sense, and so he practices it with a vengeance. He never deviates from his faithlessness; he is never guilty of charity, compassion, guilt feelings or doubts about his unbelief, or any other of the symptoms of believers, however feeble their belief; he is guilty only of slander, conspiracy, betrayal, and murder. If he admires Stavrogin, it is because he sees in Stavrogin's giant intellect even greater capacities than in himself for conspiracy, betrayal, and murder.

The position of Pyotr is nowhere better put than in his own oft-repeated statement, "I am a scoundrel, of course, and not a 'socialist,' " by which he means that he lives for himself only, not for any utopian schemes built on the sands of atheistic idealism. The only practice that can logically follow from the premise that there is no God is the practice of doing for oneself whatever can be done safely at whatever cost to others. Pyotr knows it, Stavrogin knows it, and Dostoevsky knows it. Thus Pyotr's activities are devoted solely to self-aggrandizement. He seeks power and hopes to find it through hoodwinking the utopian atheists into participating in plots and conspiracies, and eventually, in his wild imaginings, through the help of the powerful mind of Stavrogin, to overthrow the government, put Stavrogin in charge and rule from behind the scenes. His limited mind, it is true, foils his intention, and his cleverness fails him, when, having killed Shatov as a traitor to the group, he overestimates the unbelief of the conspirators.

Perhaps nowhere in the novel is Dostoevsky's exposé of atheism more devastating than the scene of the meeting of the revolutionaries called by Pyotr Verhovensky on the pretext of its being Virginsky's name-day. They all seek the earthly paradise without God, all except Stavrogin, who knows that it can't be found. He figures he's simply in the world to get the most for himself, and he has no plans to succumb to idiotic humanitarian theories and idealistic nonsense about what the future society should be like. Shigalov proposes that nine-tenths of the people be given their bread and be ruled by the other ten percent. Lyamshin, for his part, "would blow the nine-tenths of the people into the air instead of putting them in paradise." "I'd only have a handful of educated people, who would live happily ever afterwards on scientific principles," he says. And another of the members, the lame man, sums up the fashionableness of this kind of thinking: "Conversations and arguments about the future organization of society are almost an actual necessity for all thinking people nowadays. Herzen was occupied with nothing else all his life. Belinsky, as I know on very good authority, used to spend whole evenings with his friends debating and settling beforehand even the minutest, so to speak, domestic details of the social organization of the future." But Stavrogin—and Dostoevsky—know that Belinsky and Herzen have massively miscalculated the extent of man's natural goodness, and they know that Shigalov's and Lyamshin's ten percent who enjoy unbounded freedom and power, lovers of humanity all, would, in a Godless world, soon be at each others' throats. Each would want to enjoy more unbounded freedom and power than the others, until all were eliminated except one, who might then commit suicide out of boredom. Father Zossima in *The Brothers Karamazov* makes precisely this point.

Stavrogin has the capacity to convince anyone of anything. Being himself a floating atheist, spiritually unanchored, not securely able to distinguish good from bad, he juggles ideas, tossing out now this one, now that, and in the power of his intellect he wins the admiration of everyone who falls under his influence. He plentifully demonstrated the freedom of his will by engaging in all manner of perverse acts which surpass even those of the

Underground Man himself. In his perverseness, he is
capable even of charity, compassion, guilt feelings, and
twinges of religious belief. In fact, it is because he cannot
overcome his capacity to be vicitimized by his moral consciousness that he commits suicide. His needless confession to Father Tikhon that he raped a young girl who
then committed suicide, demonstrates that he could not
live with the possibility of the existence of God, and in
fact his confession is roughly the theological equivalent
of Raskolnikov's.

By contrast, Pyotr Verhovensky, the comfortable
unbeliever, does not commit suicide; he is incapable of it;
he is in this world to get from it all he can, and for him
suicide is therefore the stupidest of all acts; let suicide be
left to ideologues like Kirillov and uncomfortable
unbelievers like Stavrogin. He would gladly commit
murder; but suicide, never.

Dostoevsky underscores the horror of the atheistic
idea in *The Possessed* by putting Shatov in the most sympathetic possible position before he is exterminated by
Pyotr and his gang. It is precisely when our sympathy for
Shatov, in all his magnanimity, is at its height that he
walks into the trap set for him by Pyotr. In the course of
a single night he rejoices at the return of his wife, at the
birth of her baby (even though it is Stavrogin's), at his an-
ticipation of preaching God's word, and at the prospect
of a new life. But it is on that very night too that he, Pyotr,
"firmly and accurately put his revolver to Shatov's
forehead, pressed it to it, and pulled the trigger." Death
was almost instantaneous.

The reaction of the conspirators to the death becomes
an acid test of the intensity of their unbelief. Pyotr
himself was "the only one who preserved all his faculties"
as he searched the murdered man's pockets "with a

steady hand." But the others exposed their varying degrees of doubts about the atheistic ideal that should logically permit such a murder on the grounds that Shatov's dignity (and hence his life) was in their hands for the good of the future state. Virginsky is least faithful to the atheistic premise that brought the murder about. "It's not the right thing, it's not, it's not at all!" he cries in his shaky faithlessness. And so Pyotr has good reason to wonder whether the group will remain faithful to each other, or whether there is so much spiritual decency and righteousness, indeed religion, left in them that they would betray the others. It turns out that there is. He even fears that Kirillov's own brand of atheism is too feeble to permit him to shoot himself and thus take the blame for Shatov's murder. But fortunately Kirillov's aim, like his logic, is unerring.

By the time Dostoevsky wrote *The Possessed* he was regularly placing blame for the fruits of atheism upon the intellectuals who preached atheism, rather than those who were merely the instruments of it. In *The Possessed* the intellectual behind the scenes is Old Verhovensky, who is the most well-meaning of them all, but who, despite his doddering ineptness, is the man chiefly responsible for much of the subsequent foul play. It was he who, however unwittingly, fashioned his monster son because he did not himself know what the fruits of atheism would be.

But Dostoevsky has a special fate in store for Old Verhovensky, for in the end he does not become the victim of his ideas; rather, he is converted away from them. Like most of the "leading minds" of his time, Stepan is guilty, in Dostoevsky's view, of the two greatest intellectual crimes: belief in the natural goodness of man and disbelief in God-and-immortality. Strictly speaking,

Stepan is not a bonafide atheist, but he does not believe in any sort of personal God, much less in the God of Christianity. By this time Dostoevsky had come to recognize, however, that there is no practical difference between a deistical belief in some vague God, either pantheistic or remote, and genuine atheism: both the deist's God and the atheist's non-God lack retributive or rewarding powers, and therefore could not logically affect human behavior. "I can't understand why they make me out an infidel," says Stepan, "I believe in God, *mais distinguons*, I believe in Him as a Being who is conscious of Himself in me only. I am not a Christian." And so if Stepan is a believer he is only a technical believer; in practical terms he is as much an atheist as Pyotr and Kirillov and the others.

He is, however, an illogical atheist, for he is an idealist and he has principles. He has nothing of the understanding of Stavrogin, nor even of his son Pyotr, that if there is no God, no life after death, then virtue is meaningless and all their socialist ideals are built on sand; they have no meaning and are neither logically nor psychologically sound. Thus, it is of the utmost importance to recognize the significance of Stepan's conversion to belief in the end. Dostoevsky devotes a good deal of space to it, and since it constitutes a chief note of hope in the novel and indeed maybe Dostoevsky's main point, it deserves attention.

During his long wanderings, Stepan comes upon the gospel woman, Sonya Matveyevna, who sells Bibles. Stepan buys one from her, realizing that he had not read the gospel for at least thirty years and that he could recall some passages of it only because some seven years before he had been reading Renan's *Vie de Jésus*, one of the great anti-religious books of the 19th century. In the course of his pre-conversion illness, he tells Sonya the story of his life, during which time it is evident that he is suffering from "moral shock" and "hysterical remorse." She reads to him the Sermon on the Mount; and then in a manner presaging Dostoevsky's own death, he asks her to open the New Testament to whatever page happens to open; and so again she reads to him the passage from the Apocalypse on the subject of strong faith and no faith, which reads, "I know thy ways, that thou art neither cold nor hot; I would thou wert cold or hot. So then because thou art lukewarm, and neither cold nor hot, I will spew thee out of my mouth." From this passage Stepan concludes that it is better to be an atheist than a lukewarm believer, which is what Father Tikhon had told Stavrogin: "Complete atheism," he observed, "is more honorable than secular indifference. The complete atheist, whatever you say, still stands on the next-to-the-top step of the most perfect faith (he may step over or not), but the indifferent man has no faith whatsoever except for a bad fear, and even that only rarely, if he's a sensitive man." Stepan recognizes that in his life he has been among the lukewarm. Finally Sonya reads him another passage, this time from St. Luke, in which the devils which inhabit a possessed man enter into swine, and the herd run violently down a steep place into a lake, and are choked.

Thus does Dostoevsky alter and extend the metaphor found in *Crime and Punishment*, rendering more explicit its religious significance. The deadly microbes of atheism found infecting the minds of intellectuals in the earlier novel have become, in *The Possessed*, devils which possess those intellectuals and are then spread to the "swine," their thoughtless followers who, proceeding upon their principles, propose conspiracy and revolution. Hence the title of the novel, which is sometimes (and better) translated as *The Devils*, which, after all, constitutes the central image of the work. The point is that Stepan Verhovensky in his last hours has come to realize that his own premises lead to violent conclusions and ultimately to the destruction of the very ideas of human freedom and human dignity. The cure for the disease of atheism, as Stepan sees at last, is faith, faith in revelation, in the Bible; for the sick men, the possessed men, *can* be healed and can "sit at the feet of Christ." "My friends," Stepan says, "God is necessary to me, if only because He is the only being whom one can love eternally." And we are told that "whether he was really converted, or whether the stately ceremony of the administration of the sacrament had impressed him and stirred the artistic responsiveness of his temperament or not, he firmly, and I am told, with great feeling uttered some words which were in flat contradiction with many of his former convictions."

His chief observation on his death-bed is an affirmation of his belief in God-and-immortality, which has now become Dostoevsky's own chief message to the world. "My immortality," says Stepan, "is necessary if only because God will not be guilty of injustice and extinguish altogether the flame of love for Him once kindled in my heart. And what is more precious than love? Love is higher than existence, love is the crown of existence; and how is it possible that existence should not be under its dominance? If I have once loved Him and rejoiced in my love, is it possible that He should extinguish me and my joy and bring me to nothingness again? If there is a God, then I am immortal. *Voilà mon profession de foi.*" And so Stepan died with a hymn of praise to God on his lips, which means that, as Dostoevsky would have it, there is indeed God-and-immortality, that only the idea of God-and-immortality can assuage the injustices of life, can ultimately give a meaning to life, can indeed give a meaning, the ultimate meaning, to *The Possessed*.

Thus the theorizer of socialism, the believer in the natural goodness of man, the one who had believed that there is no God, or only an indifferent God, comes to recognize that his ideas have been wrong all along, and that he has himself been the instrument of spreading them. In the end he comes to the light of Truth in the only place in which the light of Truth is to be found, the Bible, and most clearly visible in the New Testament. And so Dostoevsky is telling us, once again, that the perfection of truth lies not in man's reason but in God's revelation, and that without *that*, there is not enough love, of the merely theoretical, unguided, random, inconstant, human sort for humanity itself to long endure.

The Raw Youth, the last of the substantial novels that preceded *The Brothers Karamazov*, is an unhappy hunting ground, full of ideas, themes, and character-types which Dostoevsky had already hashed and re-hashed; they form a mosaic in which the pieces don't fit and the colors commonly clash. Raw indeed. It seems incredible that this artistic botch which, relatively speaking, *The Raw Youth* is, could have been written on the eve of Dostoevsky's masterwork, *The Brothers Karamazov*. It is, though, the work of a mature observer and thinker, one of those great thinkers who understand men and ideas almost, if such were possible, beyond the reach of mortal men. It may therefore serve here as a harbinger of fundamental ideas which Dostoevsky expressed far more effectively in *The Brothers Karamazov*.

The spectrum of believers and unbelievers in *The Raw Youth* ranges from the spiritually alive and Chris-

tianized Makar Dolgoruky, on the one hand, to the utterly ruthless and morally anarchic Lambert on the other.
Between the two extremes are Arkady's mother, who is
religious, it seems, by instinct (and thus near to Makar),
and, toward the other end of the spectrum, the many
shades of utopian revolutionaries ranging from Vasin, the
quiet nihilist, to Kraft, who kills himself after discovering
that Russians are a "second-rate people" and that he is a
Russian. In the muddle in the middle are the spiritual
drifters, the chief characters in the novel, Versilov and
his son, Arkady.

Versilov is not an atheist, but he is no great believer
either. "I'm a deist, a *philosophe*, I suppose," he says. He
is indifferent to all the doctrines of Christianity. He
belongs to the lukewarm believers against whom the Bible speaks in the passage which the gospel-woman read
to Old Verhovensky on his death bed. He seems quite
aware of the need for belief in God-and-immortality, and
when Arkady asks him how he can make himself useful
to mankind, there is this exchange:

> "Well, I suppose discovering how to turn stones into
> bread would be a great idea."
> "The greatest idea there is? You've just pointed out a
> new goal to me. But tell me, is it really the greatest?"
> "It's very great, very great indeed, my boy, but it's not
> the greatest. In fact, it is a secondary problem and is only of
> utmost importance at the present moment, because once
> man has eaten his fill, he'll say, 'Fine, my stomach is full
> now, so what am I supposed to do next?' And that ques-
> tion remains permanently unsettled."

Here again Dostoevsky merely plays with the fundamental philosophical question: the meaning, the purpose of existence. This question becomes the core of *The
Brothers Karamazov*.

Meanwhile, Versilov's lukewarm belief and bad example do not help Arkady much in his quest for the truth, but his influence appears to have been strong enough to keep him from believing the truth. It is Arkady's ostensible father, his spiritual father, Makar Dolgoruky, who, Dostoevsky is telling us, not only possesses the truth, but believes the truth he possesses. Makar is one more in a line of truth-bearers whom Dostoevsky has by this time created. If we can believe Dostoevsky's letter to his brother, Michael, (cited on page 26, the Underground Man may have taught the truth of faith and Christ, and certainly Sonya and Bishop Tikhon taught the truth of faith and Christ as the ultimate truth. So too does Makar, who continues Dostoevsky's holy-fool tradition. Just as the Underground Man is a strange sort, and Sonya is a prostitute, and Bishop Tikhon a crazy man, Makar is a spiritual tramp, a pious pilgrim, and, for the time, a gardener. But the main thing to understand is that, whatever else Makar may be, Dostoevsky considers him to be the truthholder of the novel, and, as such, he provides a foil to the atheists, the doubters, and the spiritual drifters. As Arkady himself says of Makar, "He does believe in something solid, whereas we have nothing solid to hold onto in life."

Makar sees the world through supra-scientific eyes. "Everything's mystery, my friend," he tells Arkady, "everything is God's mystery. There's mystery in every tree, in every blade of grass. When a little bird sings or all those many, many stars shine in the sky at night—it's all mystery, the same one. But the greatest mystery is what awaits man's soul in the world beyond, and that's the truth, my boy."

But Arkady does not see life and the world in that way; in his immaturity he has a merely scientific turn of mind: "I don't quite see what you mean," he says. "Believe me, I'm not trying to tease you and, I assure you, I do believe in God. But all these mysteries you're talking about have been solved by human intelligence long ago, and whatever hasn't yet been solved will be, and perhaps very soon. The botanist today knows perfectly well how a tree grows, and the physiologist and the anatomist know perfectly well what makes a bird sing; or at least they'll know it very soon. As to the stars, not only have they all been counted, but all their movements have been calculated with an accuracy down to the last second so that it's possible to predict, say, a thousand years ahead the exact day and time of the appearance of a comet. And now even the chemical composition of the most remote stars has become known to us. . . . Also, take, for instance, a microscope, which is a sort of glass that can magnify things a million times, and look at a drop of water through it."

Whereas Dostoevsky, as referee, judges that Arkady wins the epistemological fight against the Dergachev group and their godless utopia, he also judges that Arkady loses his epistemological fight against Makar, who now proceeds to demonstrate the utter inability of science to answer the fundamental philosophical questions of existence. In response to Arkady's praise of science and man's knowledge, Makar praises religion and God's knowledge. He tells us the story of a nobleman who gives up his riches, renounces all earthly desires, and goes off to live like a monk, without, however, becoming a monk. In his search for the truth he takes with him 3,000 rubles-worth of books and a microscope. One day when Makar visits him, the nobleman shows him a drop of water under a microscope. "Here, see this drop of water that looks pure as a tear?" says the nobleman. "All right, then, look at it now and you'll see that scientists will soon explain all the mysteries of God without leaving a single one to you and me."

Arkady has his own interpretation of Makar's story. "It all seems very plain to me," he says, "Your Pyotr Valerianovich is eating his rice and raisins in his monastery and bowing to the ground while he doesn't really believe in God." But Makar sets Arkady straight by pointing out that Pyotr Valerianovich is not an atheist and that in looking at a drop of water through a microscope he is "searching for God." Such men, Makar says, are "restless." "It's all restlessness . . . for they keep on reading all their lives, and having filled themselves with bookish wisdom, they talk and talk, although they never find answers to what's bothering them and remain in the darkness. . . . A man may study all the sciences and never get rid of emptiness and gloom; indeed I think that the more intelligence he gains, the more his gloom will thicken. Life without God," he continues, "is nothing but torture. What it comes down to is that, without realizing it, they curse the only source that can brighten our life. But that won't get them anywhere because a man cannot live without worshipping something; without worshipping he cannot bear the burden of himself. And that goes for everyman. So that if a man rejects God, he will have to worship an idol that may be made of wood, gold, or ideas. So those who think they don't need God are really just idol-worshippers, and that's what we should call them."

Such is Makar's answer to those who think and live without God, and who do not feel the need of God. Even though such observations constitute the main philosophical import of the novel, they are presented in diletantish fashion and seem to have little effect upon the thought or behavior of Arkady or anyone else in the novel. Versilov floats from philosophical position to philosophical position without a rudder or an oar or a star, and so is the purveyor of many ideas but not able to distinguish the good ones from the bad ones. Arkady himself is at sea because his father is at sea, and when the novel ends he is still at sea with no port in sight or even in mind.

And yet despite five suicides, one near-suicide, half-a-dozen other deaths, several imprisonings, and deeds of vast villainy, the novel, in its last pages, appears to end happily. Versilov, though he may never marry the mother of his son, has found some sort of spiritual peace, and has apparently given up his wicked ways. The "raw youth" himself—by now cured, smoked, tenderized— has, unaccountably, set out on some sort of not-very-well-defined "new path" with the conviction that "a new life is just beginning." The extent to which Makar's thinking influenced him is, however, doubtful.

Crime and Punishment, *The Possessed*, and *The Raw Youth* all have epistemological superstructures. The basic idea in all of them, however differently expressed, is that men will never find their destiny by taking the road of reason and science; they will find it only by taking the road to God, which, it turns out, is also the road that leads through revelation and the Bible. Dostoevsky is not saying that reason and science cannot tell us important truths. He knows that they do. Razumihin, in *Crime and Punishment*, is intended as a fountain of reason and good sense. Makar himself points out, "I've always respected science, ever since I was a boy." What Dostoevsky is saying is that reason and science, which rely on merely human faculties, do not and cannot tell us the truths that finally count. It is not in the heads of Raskolnikov or Pyotr Verhovensky or Stavrogin or the Dergachev group that the key to the meaning of existence is to be found. Rather, it is to be found in the Bibles of Sonya, Bishop Tikhon, and Makar Dolgoruky. Raskolnikov and Old Verhovensky come to believe this truth in the end, and are thus on the road to regeneration. Svidrigailov, Stavrogin, Kirillov, and Kraft do not believe this truth, and end up as suicides. Arkady and Versilov only half believe it, and so, as their novel ends, they are still in a kind of spiritual limbo.

But the epistemological superstructure of *The Brothers Kramazov* towers above those of all of Dostoevsky's other novels and very likely everyone else's novels. Furthermore, *The Brothers Karamazov* marks the culmination, not only of Dostoevsky's thought, but of his art, to the point in fact that one can almost say that Dostoevsky *is The Brothers Karamazov*.

CHAPTER II

IN THE DARK

The Brothers Karamazov is so rich an encyclopedia of human experience that one can discuss it endlessly without even considering the central plot; and yet nothing in the novel is more important than the central plot. The philosophical and psychological attractions of the novel are so spectacular that one finds it easy to forget that Dostoevsky was a novelist before he was either a psychologist or a philosopher and that he therefore said what he wanted to say not by philosophizing or psychologizing but by telling stories. Even if the Legend of the Grand Inquisitor and the life and teachings of Father Zossima were omitted entirely Dostoevsky would still have said essentially what he wanted to say; but if we were left with only these celebrated sections, then most of what he wanted to say—and especially how he wanted to say it—would be lost, and lost with it would be perhaps the greatest novel ever written.

It is hard to get around the fact that the central event in the novel is the murder of Old Karamazov. But if the reader wants to solve the murder of Old Karamazov before it is solved for him, he needs to be not merely a better detective or lawyer or doctor than those in the novel, but a better philosopher. For as it turns out, those who try to solve the murder on the basis of circumstantial evidence will never do so, which is why in the end the jury sends the wrong man to prison. The murder of Old Karamazov is very likely the most philosophical murder of all time, much as Kirillov's suicide in *The Possessed* must be the most philosophical suicide of all time.

In Dostoevsky's hands the greatest conceivable philosophical significance is to be attached not only to the fact that Smerdyakov is the murderer but also that Dmitri is not the murderer. Reduced to its essence, the central question about the central plot becomes this: What point is Dostoevsky making by having Smerdyakov commit the murder when he so evidently is not the murderer, and what point is he making by having Dmitri not commit the murder when he so evidently is the murderer? The entire novel centers on these two questions; the rest, including the Grand Inquisitor scene and the life and teachings of Father Zossima, serve merely to illuminate the philosophical significance of these two facts.

Basically what Dostoevsky wanted to demonstrate is that bad ideas are vastly more destructive than bad passions, not only to individuals but to society generally and indeed to civilization itself. He wanted to show that even under the influence of the nastiest passions a man's life may be safer than under the influence of a nice atheistic idea. We are to understand that this novel is not merely about how one bad idea killed one man, any more than *Crime and Punishment* is merely about how one man killed two women. In its most universal and philosophical significance it is about how one bad idea can kill a whole civilization, for the killing of even so wicked and wretched a man as Old Karamazov by so limited a lackey as Smerdyakov symbolizes how atheism can destroy all life, including Old Karamazov's life. For atheistic ideas may have the same effect upon the whole society, indeed a whole civilization, as it may have upon one man. Dostoevsky had already made this point in two earlier novels. As Razumihin observed in *Crime and Punishment*, if Raskolnikov's idea had been more grandiose, he would have done a thousand times more harm, and in *The Possessed* Dostoevsky shows how atheism threatens civilization by letting us in on the activities of a politically-oriented organization of atheistic idealists. Atheism not only threatens lives, Dostoevsky is saying; it also threatens civilizations because it denies the sacredness of life.

On the other hand, he wanted to demonstrate also how even a slave of passion, if unmolested by atheistic notions, is less a threat to life than the cool atheist, and so he offers us a situation in *The Brothers Karamazov* in which one man, Dmitri, who virtually personified passion, is placed in a situation which makes it appear certain that he will murder his father. For almost fifty chapters Dmitri has been whipping up his passions against his father until they reach a blue heat as he lurks under his father's window observing Old Karamazov peer out into the darkness in search of Grushenka. Then comes the crucial passage:

> Mitya looked at him from the side without stirring. The old man's profile that he loathed so, his pendant Adam's apple, his hooked nose, his lips that smiled in greedy expectation, were all brightly lighted up by the slanting lamplight falling on the left from the room. A horrible fury of hatred suddenly surged up in Mitya's heart. "There he was, his rival, the man who had tormented him, had ruined his life!" It was a rush of that sudden, furious, revengeful anger of which he had spoken, as though foreseeing it, to Alyosha four days ago in the arbor, when, in answer to Alyosha's question, "How can you say you'll

kill your father?" "I don't know, I don't know," he had said then. "Perhaps I shall not kill him, perhaps I shall. I'm afraid he'll suddenly be so loathesome to me at that moment. I hate his double chin, his nose, his eyes, his shameless grin. I feel a personal revulsion. That's what I'm afraid of, that's what may be too much for me." This personal revulsion was growing unendurable. Mitya was beside himself, he suddenly pulled the brass pestle out of his pocket.

At this fateful moment Dmitri was not only suffering from the intensest kind of sexual jealousy resulting from his father's designs on Grushenka but also a consuming compulsion to get his hands on 3,000 rubles, an amount which he knew to be hidden in his father's house—in order to pay back Katerina so that he could in good conscience run off with Grushenka and begin "a new life." Such overwhelming passions in addition to the hatred of his father, who neglected him as a child, who tried to get him thrown into jail, and who otherwise tried to "ruin his life" are in themselves perhaps sufficient to drive any man to murder. Nonetheless, it is of the utmost importance to observe that what Dmitri most feared was not that he would kill his father for rational well-motivated reasons, despite the overwhelming force of those reasons, but for irrational reasons, namely "this personal revulsion," reasons which in the nature of human behavior, especially murder, are likely to be far more potent than cold-blooded, calculated reasons. Nowhere either in literature or in life was one man more liable to kill another man than Dmitri was to kill his father at that dramatic encounter described above. Why, then, after all the reader knows about the provocations and motives and inclinations and other rational and irrational signs of the most intense hatred for his father, did Dmitri not kill his father?

Dmitri himself does something to explain why he did not: "God was watching over me then," he explained on one occasion; on another he said: "Whether it was someone's tears, or my mother prayed to God, or a good angel was watching over me at that instant, I don't know. But the devil was conquered." The net meaning of Dmitri's explanation, however variously he worded it, is that some kind of religious feeling, some spiritual awareness, prevented him from carrying out the murder. During the trial the prosecutor ridicules Dmitri's claim that "pious sentiments suddenly came over him." Dmitri's attorney Fetyukovich, on the other hand, considers them seriously: "But what if there were something of the sort, a feeling of religious awe, of filial respect?" But even Fetyukovich ultimately rejects this possibility in favor of his theory that Dmitri did indeed "murder him without murdering him."

The closest we get to an accurate explanation of Dmitri's monumental feat of restraint comes from Alyosha. At the trial Alyosha admits that be believed Dmitri when Dmitri said that "in a moment of fury" he might kill his father. "But," he goes on to say, "I never doubted that *some higher feeling* [emphasis mine] would always save him at the fatal moment, as it has indeed saved him." We are to take this as a perfectly accurate account of what happened. It is Dmitri's explanation as well, and, most important, it is Dostoevsky's explanation. It is true that the prosecutor says that Alyosha's interpretation is "highly individual and contradicts all the evidence," but Dostoevsky's contempt for the prosecutor is almost as great as his contempt for the defense attorney. Most important of all, if Dmitri's heroic act of self-control cannot be explained in something like the way Alyosha explains it, then, as we shall see, the whole philosophical structure of the novel collapses.

Dostoevsky does not let the reader of *The Brothers Karamazov* know unmistakably who the murderer of the old man is until 29 chapters or, depending upon the edition, some 300 to 400 pages after it is committed. The novel is thus in the who-done-it tradition as opposed to *Crime and Punishment*, in which we not only know the murderer from the beginning but watch him carry out the crime in all its bloody details. In *Crime and Punishment*, Dostoevsky was not interested, of course, simply in "who done it"; he was interested in the philosophical and psychological and theological ramifications of murder, and he therefore wanted us to know what Raskolnikov was thinking and feeling every step of the way. The practice of withholding from the reader the identity of the murderer is characteristic of the typical who-done-it detective story because "who done it" is after all the only question the story raises and the only one it answers. On the other hand, one of the general principles of *good* story telling is *not* to withhold necessary information from the reader, on the grounds that it is more pleasurable for the reader to know something that the characters don't know than it is for the characters to know something that the reader doesn't know.

And yet Dostoevsky in *The Brothers Karamazov* is more interested in the moral and philosophical and theological meaning of murder than even in *Crime and Punishment*, and the novel itself is one of the finest stories ever told. Why, then, does he keep the reader "in the dark" about what happened in that fateful chapter entitled "In the Dark"? The answer is that he deliberately misleads the unwary reader into believing that Dmitri

killed the old man. In fact, the whole story, from the
beginning up until Chapter 8 of Book XI (entitled "The
Third and Last Interview with Smerdyakov"), which is to
say some four-fifths of the novel, is intended to mislead
the unwary reader, just as the jury and almost all of the
characters, even to the very end, are misled into believing
that Dmitri is the murderer.

And who is the unwary reader? He is the reader who
does not perceive that bad ideas are more destructive
than bad passions; more specifically he is the reader who
does not understand the consequences of atheism. In effect what Dostoevsky does is give the reader some 300 to
400 pages in which to think about who the real murderer
is, whether it is Dmitri or whether it is Smerdyakov, and
why. The wise reader, on the other hand, is the reader
who understands early on the force of atheistic ideas and
who knows that it is Ivan's cold theory that "if there is no
immortality there is no virtue and everything is lawful,"
which will lead to the death of Old Karamazov, and not
Dmitri's hot passions.

Meanwhile, Dostoevsky is playing with the reader,
and, one may suspect, is proceeding pretty fully on the
assumption that most readers will not perceive the
destructive power of atheistic ideas. This deceit is
precisely Dostoevsky's aim because when the reader does
at last know that it was Ivan's atheism and not Dmitri's
passions that are responsible for the murder, he is struck
far more forcefully by this rocking revelation than if he
had suspected all along. Ivan himself is struck so forcefully with the revelation that he goes mad.

We are to understand above all that even Ivan, who
perceived the consequences of atheism with extraordinary clarity, is by no means *fully* aware of the destruc-
tiveness of atheistic ideas until he is told by Smerdyakov

that his ideas caused his father's death. Ivan lives very un-
comfortably with the major premise of his doctrine that
"if there is no immortality there is no virtue and
everything is lawful." But only when he sees his doctrine
put into practice—when Smerdyakov kills his father—
does he see the full horror of it, a horror which drives
him over the brink.

We are not, therefore, to believe from the famous
scene between Smerdyakov and Ivan in which they
discuss the question of whether Ivan should or should not
go to Tchermashnaya that Ivan was totally aware of
what Smerdyakov was asking him, namely for permission to see to the death of his father. Ivan does not
understand the true nature of that conversation until the
chapter on "The Third and Final Interview with Smerdyakov," and therefore he did not by any means assent to
Smerdyakov's murder of his father, as is frequently supposed. It is true that he had some sort of foreboding
about that conversation, and he had some vague qualms
about it afterward, but he did not actually consent to the
murder. We are told at the end of their conversation that
he "could not have explained himself what he was feeling
at that moment," that he had "lost his bearings." He
clearly did not even understand Smerdyakov's signal, for
he almost inadvertently told Smerdyakov that he had
decided to go to Tchermashnaya. He did not even
understand what Smerdyakov meant when he said that
"It is always worthwhile speaking to a clever man."
"What did he mean by that?" Ivan asks himself, "And
why did I tell him I was going to Tchermashnaya?"

In fact one of the most important points to be made
about the novel is that Ivan learns that Smerdyakov killed
Old Karamazov by acting on Ivan's philosophical principles at precisely the same time that the reader learns it,

namely in his last interview with Smerdyakov. The whole question of Ivan's lack of awareness that Smerdyakov killed Old Karamazov appears in the simple expostulation and reply in that chapter after Smerdyakov confessed his crime:

> "Can you really not have known?" asked Smerdyakov.
> "No, I did not know," replied Ivan, "I kept thinking of my brother Dmitri."

The main plot of the novel, then, becomes an elaborate trap for the reader. Then, with the full force of his story-telling genius, Dostoevsky makes the reader perceive the horror of the consequences of atheism, specifically that an impulsive man under the spell of his passions is not nearly so dangerous as a non-contemplative man like Smerdyakov, who is under the spell of an atheistic idea.

One of the ways of looking at the structure of the novel is to consider that the main business of the plot up to the event of the murder itself is to develop potent motives for Dmitri to kill his father, and that the main business of the novel after the murder is to accumulate evidence that Dmitri did indeed kill his father.

The motives for Dmitri to kill his father are overwhelming, and they build up gradually to the description of his state of mind at the scene of the crime. Even in the early pages the reader learns that Dmitri's father neglected him as a child, that Dmitri does not like him and believes that his father is withholding from him his due patrimony. The reader learns, too, that Dmitri is "frivolous, unruly, of violent passion, impatient, and dissipated," and that when Dmitri discovered that he could get no more money from his father he was "overwhelmed, suspected deceit and cheating, and was almost beside himself." Thus, even before the reader has completed one percent of the novel, there has been laid before him the seeds of suspicion that Dmitri may do violence to his father.

The scene of the "unfortunate gathering" in Father Zossima's cell discloses further grounds for such suspicion. There Old Karamazov exposes before the whole company not only that Dmitri is in fact in debt to him—rather than vice versa—but relates the whole story of how Dmitri met Katerina, who had compromised herself in order to obtain money from Dmitri to get her father out of desperate debt, and how Dmitri, even while promising to marry Katerina, was "wasting thousands on Grushenka" and how Old Karamazov sold Dmitri's IOU's to Grushenka in order to bring about his ruin. As Miusov summarizes the situation, "A father is jealous of his son's relations with a woman of loose behavior and intrigues with the creature to get his son into prison." Dmitri and his father exchange accusations, especially over Grushenka, and the confrontation ends with Old Karamazov calling for a duel, and Dmitri calling his father "a depraved profligate, a despicable clown," and exclaiming the words of the title of the chapter, "Why is such a man alive?" "Tell me," he continues, "how can he be allowed to go on defiling the earth?" To which remark Old Karamazov replies, "Listen, listen, monks, to the parricide." Rakitin contributes to the suspicion by interpreting the mysterious gesture of Father Zossima's bowing down before Dmitri as a prediction that a terrible crime will be committed and that the criminal will be Dmitri. By this time the distinct possibility that Dmitri will kill his father is firmly planted in the reader's head.

The rivalry of Dmitri and his father for Grushenka's love is in itself enough to make Dmitri a parricide. How much does Dmitri love Grushenka? "I'll be her husband," he says, "if she will have me and when lovers come, I'll go into the next room. I'll clean her friends' galoshes, blow up their samovar, run their errands." Dmitri's passion for Grushenka is thus not of the ordinary sort; and the knowledge that his father, whom he hates as passionately as he loves Grushenka, should also be seeking her affections and is in fact willing to pay 3,000 rubles for them, or at least for a taste of them, provides this mass of emotions called Dmitri with the most perfectly poignant motive to kill Old Karamazov at the scene of the crime. The reader is reminded of this sexual jealousy often enough, and would presumably understand if Dmitri had indeed killed his father on Grushenka's account, even without the complex confluence of additional motives and emotions that have gradually built up in him.

But Dmitri's hatred for his father and his sexual passion for Grushenka are not the only motives which provoke thoughts of parricide. He also develops a mania about paying back to Katerina the 3,000 rubles he had taken from her and spent on Grushenka rather than conveying them to Katerina's sister in Moscow as she had requested. "I'd rather everyone thought me a robber and a murderer," he says. "I'd rather go to Siberia than that Katya should have the right to say that I deceived her and stole her money, and used her money to run away with Grushenka and begin a new life! That I can't do."

The fact that Dmitri needs 3,000 rubles and the fact that Old Karamazov has precisely that amount set aside to pay Grushenka if she "will come to him" is no coincidence. Here again Dostoevsky intended to lead the reader to believe that Dmitri will kill Old Karamazov to get precisely the required sum. We are to understand that the 3,000 rubles means everything to Dmitri. It is, as we are told, a matter of life and death with him, not only his life and death, but others' as well.

But Dostoevsky's deceit is to become increasingly deceitful, for shortly thereafter he provides the reader with not merely a scenario, but indeed a dress rehearsal, for the real murder. Having sent Alyosha to get 3,000 rubles from his father—hoping against hope for a "miracle"—Dmitri himself follows soon after, thinking that Grushenka is already at his father's house. When he rushes into the room, Old Karamazov cries out "He'll kill me! Don't let him get to me." Grigory, who had instructions from Old Karamazov to be on the lookout for Dmitri and to prevent him from entering, attempts to block Dmitri; but Dmitri, "beside himself with fury," hits his father with all his might (not with his pestle as he presumably did on the night of the murder, but with his fists) so that the old man "fell like a log." When he then lunges at Dmitri, Ivan cries out, "Why do you run after him? He'll murder you outright." When Dmitri returns from the bedroom where he had expected to find Grushenka, Old Karamazov shrieks: "Hold him. . . . He's been stealing money in my bedroom." Whereupon Dmitri seizes the old man by his hair, sends him crashing to the floor and kicks him "two or three times with his heel in the face." When Ivan complains, "Madman! You've killed him," Dmitri replies, "Serves him right. . . . If I haven't killed him, I'll come again and kill him. You can't protect him!"

And so, what is the reader to think upon hearing these sentiments and in following Dmitri as he starts out on a wild series of frantic misadventures in the hope that he can somehow get the 3,000 rubles to repay Katerina without having to rob and kill his father? We observe Kuzmich Samsonov's cold refusal to help Dmitri even as Dmitri points out that "it all lies in your hands! The fate of three lives and the happiness of two." We watch his mounting frustration as he tries patiently and unsuccessfully to sober up Lyagavy long enough to make him understand that he needs 3,000 rubles most desperately. And finally as he pursues his "last hope," Madame Holakhov, whom the reader finds to be funnier and crazier than ever, but who in finally declaring "I haven't a penny," causes Dmitri first to pound his fist on the table, then to spit on the floor, and finally to "burst out crying like a baby." The reader has been told that if this "last hope" were lost, "Nothing else was left him in the world but to rob and murder for the three thousand." And he now knows that there is only one more place for Dmitri to get the money, the exact amount. When he goes to Grushenka's and finds Grushenka gone, sexual jealousy is added again to all his other passions and motives, and when he picks up the pestle and rushes out the door, the reader can only echo Fenya's cry, "Oh Lord! He's going to murder someone."

Thus, when the reader comes to the passage quoted on page 52, he has been thoroughly taken in by Dostoevsky, who is in the process of demonstrating to us by the shock method how completely we underestimate the dangerous influence of atheistic intellectuals. It is as if Dostoevsky were using Dmitri's parricidal rage in order to draw attention away from where it ought to be focused, namely on Ivan's atheistic thinking as it influences Smerdyakov's action, and hence on the real cause of the murder of Old Karamazov.

But the evidence that builds against Dmitri after the murder is as overwhelming as his motives before the murder. Very few people indeed recognize his innocence, readers or characters. Alyosha speaks of "a fearful accumulation of evidence"; Grushenka cries out, "They are all, all against him, all crying out against him," and Dmitri himself observes that "the facts against me have grown numerous as the sands of the sea."

They are all reviewed at the trial, including such events as Grigory's shout of "parricide," Dmitri's clobbering Grigory with the pestle, his intention of killing himself (which might follow from his sense of guilt), the sudden appearance of much money in his pocket, though he was down to his last kopek before the murder, his offhand admission of murder to the driver who took him to Mokroë, the testimony of virtually all the witnesses, and such questions as the open door, the empty envelope, the letter to Katerina, the blood, Dmitri's strange behavior, and so on, through a 28-chapter accumulation of evidence against Dmitri until all readers, however wise or unwary, finally get confirmation that the murderer was really Smerdyakov.

The overriding reason that Dostoevsky has Dmitri deal a crushing blow to Grigory's skull is to heap up further evidence against Dmitri—the bloody hands and clothes, the confession of murder to the driver taking him to Mokroë and so on—and so further mislead the innocent reader. Even the 1,500 rubles which Dmitri kept around his neck serve, among other things, as a device to fool the reader because the reader, too, may well wonder whether Dmitri was lying about having spent only 1,500 rubles on Orgy Number One.

The whole thrust of the chapters on Dmitri's three ordeals is above all to make him look guilty, both to his questioners and to the reader. Not only is there a review in these chapters of the overwhelming circumstantial evidence against him, but there is always the suggestion that Dmitri is homicidal. We are even told, quite unfairly, that Old Karamazov was murdered "most likely with the same weapon with which Grigory had been attacked later."

Even after Ivan's second interview with Smerdyakov and only a few pages before the real murderer is unequivocally identified, Dostoevsky is still playing with the reader; for it is then that the most damaging evidence of all is presented, the evidence that was finally to convict Dmitri at the trial, namely, his fatal letter to Katerina. "I give you my word of honor," he said in the letter, "I shall go to my father and break his skull and take the money from under the pillow"; also, "I will murder the man who's robbed me!"; also, "I shall kill myself, but first of all that cur"; and again, "I am not a thief, but I'll murder my thief. Katya, don't look disdainful. Dmitri is not a thief, but a murderer,"; and finally, "Katya, pray to God that someone will give me the money. Then I shall not be steeped in gore, and if no one does I shall."

In fact well into the last interview Ivan still thinks Dmitri was the murderer, even after Smerdyakov produced the 3,000 rubles and explained how he had shammed a fit. "Stop. . . . I am getting mixed," he says to Smerdyakov; "Then it was Dmitri after all who killed him, you only took the money?" The reader too may well be "mixed," but Smerdyakov is appalled that Ivan still does not understand what really happened as the exchange quoted on page 58 of this study indicates. Ivan and the unwary reader, even up to the last moment, have not perceived that the cool unbeliever is far more dangerous to society than the hot believer.

The scene in which Ivan—and the reader—discover that Smerdyakov murdered Old Karamazov and why he murdered him is one of the most powerful discovery scenes in all literature, more powerful even than Oedipus' discovery that he had murdered his father and married his mother, or Othello's discovery of the innocence of the strangled Desdemona, and philosophically vastly more significant.

But the point is that Dostoevsky hopes that some of Ivan's sudden awareness that atheistic ideas have consequences will rub off on those readers who, along with almost all the characters, have been deceived by mere circumstantial evidence. More specifically, Dostoevsky hopes that the reader too will begin to see the truth of Ivan's slogan that "If there is no immortality, there is no virtue and everything is lawful," and that even in the most passionate heart there may remain fits of decency, if unmolested by atheistic influences, that can turn a man away from crime even under the worst possible circumstances.

But while Dostoevsky is engaging in all this deceit he provides plenty of hints along the way so that the reader need by no means be wholly taken in by the overwhelming evidence against Dmitri. The first, and in some ways the most obvious hint occurs immediately after Dmitri pulls the pestle out of his pocket as if to strike his father. The narrative breaks off at this point with a hiatus and then takes up again with the words, " 'God was watching over me then', Mitya himself said afterwards." The reader may convince himself from these enigmatic words that Dmitri did not kill his father after all, though he cannot, at this point, so easily guess that Smerdyakov was the murderer, much less why.

Perhaps the most helpful hints come from an understanding of Dmitri's character, which I will discuss at length in the next chapter, and hence from his repeated protestations of innocence; for whether the reader realizes it or not, Dostoevsky is asking for great faith in Dmitri's innocence, just as Grushenka and Alyosha themselves have great faith in his innocence. But great faith indeed is required. The fact is that almost every other character in the novel, including Dmitri's own defense attorney, believes he is guilty.

One must also answer the question, Why are Alyosha and Grushenka (and Kolya's little friend Smurov) so certain that Dmitri did not murder his father? Madame Holakhov, it is true, has the distinction of believing, at least at one time, that Grigory is the murderer but literally everyone else, including Ivan (until the last interview with Smerdyakov), Katerina, Rakitin, Kalganov, Grigory, Dr. Herzenstube, the "Moscow doctor," Doctor Vavinsky, the prosecuting attorney, the defense attorney, the court officials, Perhotin, Fenya, the Poles, Trifon Borissevitch, all the spectators at the trial, and doubtless everybody else who read about the trial, which was reported all over Russia, and above all the jury which convicted him, are convinced that Dmitri is the murderer.

What do Alyosha and Grushenka know that they don't know, indeed that the reader doesn't know? It turns out that what they know has nothing to do with circumstantial evidence however conclusive it may seem to be. What they know, they know "in their hearts," and chiefly from what they know about human nature in general and Dmitri's nature in particular. It is quite true that they do not have any understanding of the influence that Ivan's ideas worked upon Smerdyakov, but they do know something that the reader also knows, however easily he may be misled by the incriminating evidence, namely that Dmitri is basically an honorable man whose thinking has not driven out his religious instincts.

The main point to be made about the trial scene is that when it is all over and Dmitri has been found guilty, there is only one person in the entire courtroom who knows exactly what happened on that fateful night and why (Smerdyakov having hanged himself) and that is Ivan; and he is hauled out of the court kicking and screaming and pronounced a madman. Not even Dmitri knows exactly why the murder happened, nor does Alyosha. Every other character in the courtroom is convinced that Dmitri is the murderer, including even Dmitri's own lawyer, who in effect enters a plea of guilty with a request for mercy. The only others who know what Ivan knows are the readers of the novel, and so they can feel not only a knowing superiority over all the unwary characters but also a lacerating compassion for Dmitri, who hears the jury reply, "Yes, guilty" to every charge without the slightest extenuating comment. Dostoevsky has carefully calculated these emotional reactions of the reader because he wants above all for the reader to understand not only the horrible consequences of atheistic ideas, but also the essential decency of the human heart.

When all the circumstantial evidence has been viewed and reviewed, the prosecuting attorney says, "Show us a single fact in the prisoner's favor and we will rejoice," and the defense attorney replies with equal assurance that even though "there is an overwhelming chain of evidence against the prisoner . . . at the same time not one fact will stand criticism if it is examined separately." Actually, both are right. All the elaborate testimony of all the witnesses, the speculation about the various kinds of damaging evidence, such as the bloody clothes, the 3,000 rubles, the open door, the empty envelope, even Dmitri's letter to Katerina, all are quite beside the point. No one in the case really knows the facts, the doctors and lawyers least of all, because none understands the workings of the human soul. They are not interested in the workings of the human soul and they do not even come close to understanding the destructive power of atheism.

The fact that the statements of both the prosecuting and the defense attorneys are true does something to demonstrate that Dostoevsky is not dealing ultimately in pestles and pistols or in blood or open doors or letters or rubles, but in ideas, and he is telling the reader that conclusions about Dmitri's guilt or innocence must be made on purely philosophical grounds and upon the workings of the human heart, not on the grounds of circumstantial evidence and palpable fact. In the novel, however, Dmitri is tried by circumstantial evidence and palpable fact, and so is wrongly convicted. The reader, on the other hand, is forced into a corner and obliged to make his judgment upon philosophical grounds. The trial is merely a matter of going through the motions. It turns up nothing that really helps. It is the human soul that is on trial, and that cannot be judged in a courtroom.

What then is the significance of the discussions about God-and-immortality that take up not only most of Books V and VI of the novel, but a good deal of the rest of the novel too in one way or another? These parts of the book are not digressions; they turn out to support the philosophical meaning of the central plot of the novel, and it is the speculation about the consequences of whether God-and-immortality exist or not that the reader should have been paying attention to, not the pistols and pestles and blood and rubles and letters and open doors.

In the epilogue Alyosha tells us that Ivan is "lying at death's door"; he may recover, and if he does, then he may tell Alyosha and Katerina and Grushenka and Dmitri and everyone else what really happened on that fateful night and why, and then they too will have something of the insight into the consequences of atheism that Ivan had and that drove him mad. On the other hand, he may die, and then they will never know. Meanwhile, however, the reader knows, and it is the reader's knowing that counts, not the characters' in a novel, and that is what Dostoevsky wanted to achieve.

CHAPTER III

DMITRI: THE SINNING BELIEVER

Dostoevsky explored the outer limits of human behavior because he knew that the true nature of man
can be understood only if the outer limits of his behavior
can be understood. Before Dostoevsky, our best novelists
were hardly aware of the sado-masochistic aspects of
mankind that interested Dostoevsky, nor could they portray either human degradation or spiritual heroics with
anything like Dostoevsky's power and perception. The
Underground Man's professional perverseness, for example, overwhelms us with evidence of the existence and
necessity of free will. Prince Myshkin's goodness is so
good that we think of him as an idiot; and Kirillov enjoys
the unique experience of killing himself in order to
demonstrate that God does not exist. One can cite
endless examples of the extremes of human behavior in
Dostoevsky's art.

Needless to say, they are plentiful in *The Brothers
Karamazov*. The three brothers themselves admirably illustrate the phenomenon, for all of them are in their way
supermen and all of them strike awe in the heart of the
reader. Ivan is the intellectual superman, whose giant intellect enables him to understand the consequences of
unbelief to a greater extent perhaps than even the most
powerful intellectuals in the world today. Alyosha

possesses enough spiritual faith to qualify him as a spiritual superman, even though in one place he falters and even though in his youthfulness he is overshadowed by the super-spirituality of the aged Father Zossima.

But it is Dmitri as the emotional superman who provides us with perhaps the most spectacular combination of good deeds and dirty deeds done by one man in the whole history of the novel. He is indeed, as the prosecutor Ippolit Kirillovitch observed of him, "a marvellous mingling of good and evil." His dirty deeds are in the grand Dostoevsky tradition, and include such choice feats as: (1) proposing to seduce Katerina, the virtuous and lovely Katerina, in return for 4,000 rubles which she desperately needs in order to save her father from disaster; (2) taking 3,000 rubles entrusted to him by Katerina, then his fiancée, to take to her sister, and squandering them instead on two orgies with his girlfriend, Grushenka; (3) humiliating Captain Snegiryov in front of his little son by pulling him out of a tavern by his beard; (4) rushing into his father's house, sending him crashing to the floor, and kicking him repeatedly in the face with his heel, and promising to return to kill him in earnest; and (5) smashing Grigory's head with a pestle so that Grigory's recovery approaches the miraculous.

Dmitri is also both suicidal and homicidal. He makes determined plans to kill himself as a result of the mess he got himself into with Katerina and Grushenka. He also at one time or another threatens to kill Smerdyakov, and even Fenya, and according to Grushenka's servants, he even threatened to kill her. He is forever threatening to kill his father and on one occasion came fairly close to doing so; and he thought with very good reason that he indeed killed Grigory. He is moreover a diligent student of assorted vices such as drinking, gambling, and whoring, and he has one of the most terrible tempers of all time. Dostoevsky himself tells us that he was "irascible by nature" to the point in fact of being "of an unstable and unbalanced mind."

But if Dmitri is forever exercising his bad passions, he is also forever exercising his good heart, often in no less awesome a manner. For example : (1) When Katerina in all her delicious beauty comes for the 4,000 rubles he finds himself panting to the point of swooning, and yet his impulsive high-mindedness prevents him from seducing her after all, even though he still lends her the money; (2) he is so bent on restitution for the abominable misuse of the 3,000 rubles that Katerina had entrusted to him in his confusion he is willing to murder his father to pay it back; (3) even though he had resolved to kill himself, he decides, like the hero of *The Dream of a Ridiculous Man*, not to kill himself after all but to dedicate his life to loving and helping others even in a Siberian prison camp; (4) he does not kill his father despite the most overwhelming provocations and passions imaginable but instead by a truly heroic act of restraint permits God to stay his hand; and (5) most heroic of all, he accepts the sentence to Siberia for a crime he did not commit as the opportunity to expiate the crimes that he did commit.

Furthermore, we are told over and over again that Dmitri is basically a man of honor. He himself says that he is a man of honor. "You have to deal with a man of honor," he reminds his interregators, "A man of the highest honor; above all don't lose sight of it—a man who's done a lot of nasty things but has always been, and still is honorable in his being." We also have the word of a good many others in the novel that Dmitri is a man of character and honor. Dr. Hertzenstube, Police Captain Mikhail Mikhailovich, and Katerina all recognize in him an honorable and good heart. Alyosha describes him as "violent-tempered perhaps and carried away by his passions, but at the same time honorable, proud, and generous, capable of self-sacrifice, if necessary." Perhaps the most significant estimate of Dmitri's character comes from the peasant who drove him to Mokroë: "you're like a child . . . that's how we look on you . . . and though you're hasty tempered, sir, yet God will forgive your kind heart." In these words we may have Dostoevsky's own judgment of Dmitri.

But what makes Dmitri's good deeds and dirty deeds meaningful is his spiritual progress, and the meaning of that spiritual progress can be best understood against a background of the entire spiritual spectrum of the novel, which I should like therefore briefly to examine.

Dostoevsky's chief aim in Book II entitled "An Unfortunate Gathering," apart from the obvious one of introducing the *dramatis personae* and the ostensible one of attempting to settle Dmitri's financial accounts with his father, is to define at the outset the spiritual spectrum over which man is capable of ranging from assiduous atheism to boundless belief.

At one end is Father Zossima, a man of infinite faith in the truth of Christ, who in his hard-won saintliness has not only achieved a wondrous spiritual peace and inner happiness but has developed uncanny powers to detect the spiritual troubles of others and hence has achieved a wide reputation as spiritual adviser. In fact, Dostoevsky uses Father Zossima as the yardstick to measure the spiritual deficiencies of all the other characters who attend the unfortunate gathering, in something of the same way that Prince Myshkin in his saintliness serves to measure the spiritual weaknesses of all the other characters in *The Idiot*.

Dostoevsky illustrates the attitude toward religion of all the visitors to the monastery by their attitude toward Father Zossima and particularly by the way in which they greet him. When Father Zossima enters the cell, the monks rise, bow deeply, touch the ground with their fingers and then kiss his hand "with the appearance of feeling, not like an everyday rite." Miusov, on the other hand, in his imperception, is convinced of the falseness of the monks' feelings for Father Zossima and he leads the parade of unbelievers by refusing to kiss his hand, as was customary, but merely offered "a rather deep conventional bow," and then moved back to a chair. Old Karamazov does the same and characteristically mimics Miusov, like an ape. Ivan, who was next, and who, like Miusov, attended the gathering merely "from curiosity, perhaps the coarsest kind," "bowed with great dignity and courtesy but he too kept his hand at his sides." Kalganov, the prospective novice, who is undecided about his spiritual future, was so confused by the gestures and omissions of the others that he did not even bow.

Thus the breadth of the spiritual spectrum of the novel, and indeed of mankind, is established. There is the feeling unbelief of Rakitin and Miusov and Old Karamazov, which is not merely comfortable but cozy, and which thus makes them guilty of the worst offense in the Christian code, namely spiritual pride; there is the doubting unbelief of Ivan, which makes him perhaps the most uncomfortable atheist either in literature or in life; there is the devoutness of Alyosha, who had already decided: "I want to live for immortality, and I will accept no compromise," and who thus, under Father Zossima's tutelage, is already well on his way to holiness; there are the monks, including Father Paissey, who have already achieved something of a state of holiness out of firm belief; and finally, there is Father Zossima, who in his saintly state has earned the rightful reverence of most, the jealousy of a few, like the overrighteous Father Ferapont, and the contempt of easy unbelievers like Miusov.

Other characters, as the novel unfolds, enrich the spiritual spectrum. Smerdyakov in his dullness learned his comfortable atheism from Ivan, the uncomfortable atheist. Kolya swings from a shallow atheism under Rakitin's guidance to a Christian belief in God-and-immortality under Alyosha's guidance. Dostoevsky's women are not much given to religious thought, though they exhibit a great deal of good will as well as ill will, and both Grushenka and Katerina suffer exquisite spiritual torments on account of their consciences and senses of guilt. Madame Holakhov, having pronounced herself a woman of little faith, goes to Father Zossima for spiritual help and thereby strains his skill to the limit, and perhaps beyond. Liza, too, suffers from her own peculiar spiritual torments.

But where does Dmitri fit into this spiritual spectrum? He has none of the spiritual discipline and religious dedication of Alyosha, nor, on the other hand, has he been talked out of his religion by learning or by his unaided reason, like Ivan. He is without the spiritual training of Alyosha that perfects his faith, or the intellectual training of Ivan that has destroyed his. His emotions are polluted by destructive instincts, but his mind is not polluted by atheistic ideas.

The initial clue to Dmitri's religious inclinations comes from his entrance into Father Zossima's cell, whom he had never seen before. He "went straight up to the elder," we are told, "made him a low bow," and asked his blessing. Father Zossima blessed him, and

Dmitri "kissed his hand respectfully." The contrast between Dmitri's manner of greeting Father Zossima and that of the atheistic guests is telling.

But a detailed account of Dmitri's credo comes in the chapter entitled "The Confession of a Passionate Heart— In Verse," which constitutes a kind of philosophical prelude to his confession to Alyosha of his troubles with Katerina and Grushenka. Dmitri admits to Alyosha that he has sunk into the vilest degradation and in fact is so ashamed that he breaks into sobs. And yet, "in the very depths of that degradation," he tells Alyosha, "I begin my hymn of praise. . . . Though I may be following the devil, I am Thy son, O Lord, and I love Thee, and I feel joy without which the world cannot stand."

Thus the reader is made aware of Dmitri's religious orientation, his awareness of God, of Christ, and of his own spiritual nature,—as well as his ignoble nature. He has a simple faith, an unenlightened faith, but a sincere and in some ways a deep faith. As the novel proceeds it becomes deeper and more sophisticated—and indeed crucial to his very survival.

Dmitri's story becomes a dramatic contest to determine whether the despair to which his passions are leading him will be conquered by the hope to which his religion is leading him. God and the Devil never fought harder for anyone's heart, perhaps, than for Dmitri's. That is what Father Zossima perceived and that is why he so dramatically—and to the puzzlement of all— bowed down before him in the monastery.

For as Dmitri's story develops, the gap between his beliefs and his actions widens. Both the ideal of the Madonna in him and the ideal of Sodom become increasingly active, and the wedge that is being thrust between them is the 3,000 rubles which Dmitri has vowed to return to Katerina. He vows "to move heaven and earth" to return the money, and if worse comes to worst he will kill his father for that exact sum, which he knows to be hidden in his father's house as a lure for Grushenka.

But to this combination of bad passions which lead Dmitri to resolute thoughts of robbery and murder, he also adds thoughts of suicide, which on three different occasions he almost carries out. Especially after hitting Grigory over the head and leaving him for dead, he is ready to give up the world. He needs above all to conquer the giant Despair, and Dostoevsky gives us to understand that victory cannot be achieved with the skinny stick of Reason, but only with the spiked club of Faith.

But his faith is still very much alive, for when he learns that Grigory has in fact recovered, he offers a prayer of thanksgiving: "Lord, I thank thee for this miracle Thou hast wrought for me, a sinner and evildoer. That's an answer to my prayer, I've been praying all night." And he crosses himself three times. The news lifts a terrible burden from his soul, to the point, in fact, that "he seemed completely transformed in a moment"; and upon realizing that he is no more a murderer than his interrogators, he once again feels himself their equal, even as the "terrible facts" against him accumulate.

After the interrogators have finished their tortuous questioning, at one point even forcing him to take off all his clothes, he is exhausted and lies down and at once falls asleep. He dreams a dream which is the real beginning of his spiritual transformation. It is about a hungry babe, its clothes frozen and its fists blue from the cold, crying as it is held by the dark-faced mother, whose hut, and indeed half of whose village, has been burned. The dream is so powerful that it leads him to the revelation that "all are responsible for all." When he awakens, there is "a new light, as of joy, on his face." He summons Alyosha to tell him about his dream, this "blow from heaven," that caused him to find in himself "a new man." "A new man has risen up in me," he tells Alyosha; "He was hidden in me but would never have come to the surface if it hadn't been for this "blow from heaven. Never, never should I have risen of myself! But the thunderbolt has fallen."

It is out of this revelation that he accepts his Siberian sentence, despite his innocence in his father's death. "It's for the babe, I'm going," he tells Alyosha, "for all the 'babes', For there are big children as well as little children. All are 'babes'. I go for all because someone must go for all. I didn't kill my father, but I've got to go. I accept it. It's all come to me here within these peeling walls."

It is especially important to recognize that Dmitri's spiritual transformation has withstood the satanic temptations of Rakitin. Rakitin, with all the characteristic imperceptions of the comfortable atheist, visits him in his cell with the purpose of writing an article demonstrating that Dmitri couldn't help murdering his father because he was corrupted by his environment. But during the course of these visits Rakitin regales Dmitri with the by-then common atheist-materialist line that man is nothing but matter in motion and that what distinguishes man from beasts is mere reason. Man's essence, says Rakitin, is in the 'little tails' which make up the nerves of the brain, and it is these little quivering tails, that is, man's reason, which constitute the essence of man, rather than his soul, which in fact he does not have; nor is he made in the image of likeness of God, for there is no God either.

But Dmitri, in a mocking vein, abundantly demonstrates his contempt for Rakitin's theories: "Rakitin explained it all to me yesterday," he tells Alyosha, "and it simply bowled me over. It's magnificent, Alyosha, this science! A new man's arising—that I understand—It's chemistry, brother, chemistry! There's no help for it, your reverence, you must make way for chemistry." Dmitri gets to the heart of the problem of Rakitin's thinking by perceiving at once in his simple way the same truth that Ivan perceived in a grand way: "But what will become of man, then, I asked him 'without immortal life'?" Rakitin's reply is the logical reply of the logical atheist: "Didn't you know," said Rakitin laughing, "a clever man can do what he likes." And indeed the highest logical virtue of the logical atheist is cleverness, the cleverness to do what is in one's own private interests without getting caught by authorities in a world still inhabited by imperfect unbelievers. "A clever man knows his way about," he tells Dmitri, "but you've put your foot in it, committing a murder, and now you are rotting in prison." Rakitin sees nothing wrong in murdering Old Karamazov if one can get away with it, and if it is to one's advantge, or in stealing 3,000 rubles from Katerina. Rakitin himself, in his cleverness, has in mind to marry poor old feeble-minded Madame Holakhov for her 15,000 rubles. But as Dostoevsky would point out, if there is no God-and-immortality, then Rakitin's position is not merely logical, it is unassailable.

For Dmitri, on the other hand, the crime of taking 3,000 rubles from his fiancée and lavishing it on his girlfriend weighs so heavily on his mind that it's all he can do to keep from killing himself in despair; and as for the murder, he tells his interrogators that if he had killed his father, he would have felt so terrible that he would have committed suicide on the spot. Dostoevsky's point is that Dmitri's suffering and despair are logical only if there is

God-and-immortality; otherwise Rakitin and his doctrine of cleverness are right and Dmitri and his doctrine
of suffering are wrong.

As Dmitri himself puts the problem, "What if Rakitin's right—that God is an idea made up by men? Then,
if He doesn't exist, man is the chief of the earth, of the
universe. Magnificent! Only how is he going to be good
without God? That's the question. I always come back to
that. For whom is man going to love then? To whom will
he be thankful? To whom will he sing the hymn? Rakitin
says that one can love humanity without God. Well, only
a snivelling idiot can maintain that."

Thus Dmitri rejects Rakitin's doctrine of cleverness
and instead gives himself to Christ and His doctrine of
suffering. "We shall be in chains and there will be no
freedom," he tells Alyosha. "But then, in our great sorrow,
we shall rise again in joy, without which man cannot live,
nor God exist, for God gives joy."

What is important about Dmitri, so far as Dostoevsky is concerned, is not whether he remains in Siberia or
escapes to America, but rather whether his belief con-
quers his passions, whether the Madonna overcomes the
Sodom in him, whether his hope overcomes his despair.
It is in this crucial scene with Alyosha in prison that
Dmitri's spiritual struggles are resolved. And they are
resolved in God's favor, in much the same way, as we
shall see, that the spiritual struggles of the young
Zossima were resolved and even the spiritual struggle of
his brother Markel, who exerted a potent spiritual influence on Zossima. For ultimately, Dostoevsky is saying
that if Dmitri and every other despairing soul is to be
saved from despair, it will not be by reason but by revelation, not by philosophy but by religious faith.

CHAPTER IV

IVAN *AGONISTES*

Ivan is the uncomfortable atheist *par excellence*. The source of his discomfort is his exquisite understanding of the consequences of unbelief not only to himself but also to civilization, and yet he cannot believe. Like Dostoevsky himself, Ivan recognizes the awful truth, repeated over and over again in the novel, that "If there is no immortality there is no virtue and everything is lawful."

Miusov as a disciple of the Enlighteners sneers at Ivan's conclusion, but Father Zossima perceives at once that Ivan has got directly to the heart of the question of the importance of God-and-immortality to civilization. "Is that really your conviction as to the consequences of the disappearance of faith and immortality?" he asks; and when Ivan replies, "yes, that was my conviction," then Father Zossima tells him, "You are blessed in believing that or else most unhappy." He would be blessed if he believed in immortality because Father Zossima knows it as "the loftiest idea of human existence," but he perceives that Ivan has doubts about immortality, and he therefore knows that he is most unhappy. "The question is still fretting your heart," he tells him. "The martyr likes sometimes to divert himself with his despair. . . . In your despair, you too divert yourself with magazine articles, and discussions in society, though you don't believe your own arguments, and with an aching heart mock at them inwardly. . . . That question you have not answered, and it is your great grief, for it clamors for an answer."

But Zossima also consoles Ivan in his spiritual suffering: "Thank the Creator who has given you a lofty heart capable of suffering," he tells him, "of thinking and seeking higher things, for our dwelling is in the heavens. God grant that your heart will attain the answer on earth." By the time the novel has ended, Ivan's heart has indeed, as we shall see, attained the answer on earth.

One of the articles with which Ivan diverted himself in his despair is the one on church government, in which he points out that the State ought to become the Church. If the end of life is salvation, he argues, then the Church knows the best way to achieve it and so the State should be transformed into the Church. It is for this reason that Father Paissey in an act of perfect faith cries out, "So be it! So be it!" which are the words of the chapter title.

But as Ivan knows, the faith of man is imperfect because men themselves are imperfect, so imperfect that in practice the idea of the State becoming the Church is preposterous because neither trusts the other. In fact the extent to which neither trusts the other is merely a measure of the imperfection of men's faith, and the more outraged the reader is at Ivan's proposal the more the reader demonstrates his own lack of faith. Not many can sincerely echo Father Paissey's words, and Ivan knows it; and that is what Ivan wanted to show: namely that there is very little faith in the world. The article is thus an exercise in logic, but it is at the same time a devastating exposé of faithlessness in the Christian world.

I should like for a moment to explore the roots of Ivan's spiritual dilemma because much of the meaning of the novel depends upon an understanding of it. As the prosecutor Ippolit Kirilovitch observed of Ivan, he is "one of those modern young men of brilliant education and vigorous intellect who has lost faith in everything," chiefly because of his "adoption of European ideas." The chief European idea that Ivan has adopted is the Enlighteners' idea that revelation, specifically the divine origin of the Scriptures is not a valid means to truth, and that mere human reason must take its place. In other words, like the Enlighteners, Ivan has lost his faith. When he tells Alyosha that he cannot accept God's world, he in effect is saying that he can't accept anything that is supra-rational or that violates his reason, including the supernatural basis of the Scriptures. "Even if parallel lines do meet, and I see it myself," he says, "I shall see it and say they've met, but still I won't accept it. That's what's at the root of me, Alyosha, that's my creed." Ivan has become a victim of the tyranny of mere reason.

Yet he cannot bring himself to accept the vast faith in natural man which was the cornerstone of the teachings of the Enlighteners and of their successors, the full-blown Romantics. He does not suppose that mere human reason would lead men to goodness any more than Dostoevsky did, and he is even less inclined to believe with the Romantics that human instincts and emotions more surely than reason are the key to virtue and hence to happiness.

In fact, if anything, Ivan has too low an estimate of man in his natural state, indeed an almost Hobbesian view. When Alyosha observes that "there is a great deal of love in mankind, an almost Christ-like love," Ivan replies, "Well, I know nothing of it so far, and can't understand it." In comparing children to adults, Ivan observes that adults are "disgusting and unworthy of love," that they've eaten the apple and know good and evil, and they have become "like God. They go on eating it still." Ivan believes, too, that it is "almost impossible" to love one's neighbors except in the abstract or at a distance because men's disposition to great goodness is so slight. A beast, he says, "can never be so cruel as a man, so artistically cruel. The tiger only tears and gnaws, that's all he can do. He would never think of nailing people by the ears, even if he were able to do it." With these last words Ivan proceeds, in the chapter entitled "Rebellion," to regale Alyosha with a string of stories about adults who maimed and killed children in the most horrible ways, the source of which stories Dostoevsky himself had gleaned from newspaper clippings.

Thus Ivan perceives that if indeed there is no God, or only the God that mere human reason can fashion, and if men are as ill-disposed to goodness as he insists, and as broad experience and the history of mankind would tend to verify, how, then, to use Dmitri's words, "How is he going to be good without God?" Ivan has already indicated what a world of natural unbelieving men would become if belief in God-and-immortality were to be destroyed; "not only love but every living force maintaining the life of the world would at once be dried up," he says. "Moreover, nothing then would be immoral, everything would be lawful, even cannibalism." That is why Ivan observes that if God did not exist Man would have to invent him, and why he says that "there would have been no civilization if they hadn't invented God."

Ivan sees with crystal clarity the necessity of belief, in a world inhabited by "fallen men." He also perceives that without God-and-immortality every "evil action," however whimsical, may be performed with absolute impunity so long as one does not get caught. He also recognizes with sorrow that love either of individuals or of mankind in general has no meaning beyond the pleasure and satisfaction it brings the lover, that love is no more a virtue than hatred is a vice, that all morality logically collapses and that there should be no logical distinction between a human ethic and a beast ethic. And still he cannot believe.

And yet, Ivan is not a truly logical atheist: on the contrary, he is a virtuous atheist. He is a man not only of the greatest decency and honor but of the highest principles. One of the best ways of understanding the gap between his beliefs and his behavior is to compare him to Old Karamazov and to Smerdyakov, both of whom believe quite comfortably that there is no immortality and who, in their indisputable logic, can act as if there were no virtue and that everything is lawful.

Old Karamazov had apologized to Alyosha for his abominable behavior at the monastery, observing that "If there is a God, if He exists, then, of course, I'm to blame, and I should have to answer for it." "But," he continues, "if there isn't a God at all, what do they deserve, your fathers? It's not enough to cut their heads off, for they keep back progress." Old Karamazov recognizes that he is taking a gamble in believing that there is no God, but having gambled, he plays the game of life to the hilt. "I mean to go on in my sins to the end," he tells Alyosha. "For sin is sweet; all abuse it, but all men live in it, only others do it on the sly, and I openly. And so all the other sinners fall upon me for being so simple. And your paradise, Alexei Fyodorovitch, is not to my taste, let me tell you that; and it's not the proper place for a gentleman, your paradise, if it exists. I believe that I shall fall asleep and won't wake up again, and that's all. You can pray for my soul if you like, and if you don't want to, don't, damn you! That's my philosophy."

If there is no immortality, there is an indisputable logic to Old Karamazov's philosophy. Why should he not continue in his hedonistic ways? He wants to save all his money so that "when wenches won't come to him of their own accord," he will have money to pay them to come, especially 20 years later when he reaches age 75. Society doesn't care how much he pays his wenches to come to him or at what age or how often, or whether he gets them free or whether he pays Grushenka 3,000 rubles. Meanwhile, Old Karamazov has all the courage of his convictions. Orgies are a way of life with him, and except for his first wife, an exceptionally beautiful girl, for whom, ironically, he could work up no passion, he could and did lust after every woman he ever saw, including Stinking Lizaveta, the ugly, deformed idiot girl, upon whom he begot Smerdyakov. And as a logical atheist why should he not enjoy even her? The experience would be rare, even unique, and could be carried out with impunity, or at least theoretically it could. It was simply an irony, a bit of cosmic irony, that in Old Karamazov's case the offspring of his lust for Stinking Lizaveta should rise up and crush his skull one night with a paperweight.

Old Karamazov marvellously summed up his own philosophy: "We clever people will sit snug and enjoy our brandy." He observes Alyosha and other believers denying themselves such pleasures of life as are crucial to Old Karamazov's unbelieving being. Ivan told Dmitri that his father is a pig, but that "his ideas are right enough." But Old Karamazov is a pig precisely because he does act according to his ideas. Ivan is not a pig precisely because he cannot. Ivan and Old Karamazov epitomize respectively the virtuous atheist and the logical atheist.

Smerdyakov is another comfortable unbeliever, though he acts on the courage of Ivan's convictions, which he interprets in his own way. For Smerdyakov, as for Old Karamazov and Rakitin, the great virtue is "cleverness," and by the "clever" man he means the unbeliever who can act solely with a view to his own self-interest or pleasure in such a way as not to get caught in a world that still believes in virtue. Virtuous men he regards as stupid, whereas "clever" men can do a great deal that virtuous men are afraid to do because they believe in God-and-immortality or are conditioned by a society that does, or at least once did. Smerdyakov's philosophy is therefore, as he says, to "hoodwink the fools." In the dimness of his understanding he takes Ivan's statement that "if there is no immortality, there is no virtue and everything is lawful" out of the conditional and puts it into the declarative and so kills Old Karamazov.

Thus when one compares the *sang-froid* with which Smerdyakov kills Old Karamazov with the horror that strikes Ivan upon learning that Smerdyakov had in fact killed Old Karamazov using Ivan's own ideas, the fundamental decency of Ivan comes through, as does the intensity of his spiritual agony. Despite what his logic tells him, he is, unlike Smerdyakov, caught by his conscience. "What is conscience!" he exclaims. "Why am I tormented by it? From habit. From the universal habit of mankind for seven thousand years. So let us give it up and we shall be gods."

Ivan's conscience, which he owes to the influence of religion, the validity of which he denies but the necessity of which he admits, makes him a truly decent and

honorable man—and the spiritually tortured man.
"Don't condemn me, and don't look on me as a villain,"
he tells Alyosha, and Alyosha does not. Ivan's behavior is
not only not condemnable but heroic; it is his ideas that
wreak destruction. He is heroic precisely because against
all logic he acts in opposition to his beliefs.

The fact that Ivan is so utterly shocked upon learning
that Smerdyakov killed his father ought to be evidence
enough that he was not consenting to his murder earlier
in the book in talking to Smerdyakov about the Tchermashnaya business. In fact, when it finally becomes clear
to Ivan that Smerdyakov is the murderer, his first instinct
ironically is to kill Smerdyakov on the spot. But having
come to realize that atheistic *ideas* can murder as well as
people, he proposes to take Smerdyakov to the trial the
next day with the understanding that they will confess
together. "The only reason I haven't killed you is that I
need you for tomorrow," Ivan tells Smerdyakov, and he
vows that if Smerdyakov will not testify he will testify
alone. He wants to make a clean breast of it all, to take
the blame, or at least part of the blame. In fact he
becomes conscious of an "unbounded resolution" to
testify at the trial on the next day that not Dmitri but he
and Smerdyakov are the guilty ones.

Smerdyakov in his comfortable unbelief takes a
logically cynical view of Ivan's human nature. "You
won't go to give evidence," he says. "It isn't possible. You
are very clever. You are fond of money. I know that. You
like to be respected too, for you're very proud; you are
far too fond of female charms, too, and you mind most
of all about living in undisturbed comfort, without having to depend on anyone—that's what you care most
about. You won't want to spoil your life forever by taking such a disgrace on yourself. You are like Fyodor

Pavlovich, you are more like him than any of his children; you've the same soul as he had."

This is the argument that should have won Ivan over completely because it is the logical, indeed the inevitable, conclusion to which Ivan's unbelief ought to lead. It is the unassailable logic of the logical, the clever, atheist. But Smerdyakov is dead wrong about Ivan, not only in his supposition that Ivan regards comfort as the *summum bonum*, but also in comparing him to Old Karamazov. It is precisely because he is not like his father and because he does not consider comfort the *summum bonum*, despite his philosophy, that he suffers all manner of spiritual torments, and none so tormenting as the one that now faces him. Alyosha said of Ivan, early in the novel, "It's not comfort Ivan is seeking. Perhaps it's suffering he's seeking." But as Dostoevsky keeps telling us, if there is no immortality then it is utter folly to seek suffering, or even to pursue goodness.

But the worst of Ivan's spiritual agonies are yet to come. If there is no God-and-immortality, he would be, as Smerdyakov suggests, a damned fool to give himself up because he could go to his grave without anyone ever knowing that he was in any way the cause of his father's death. And yet his incorrigible decency and honor and conscience and insistence upon facing the truth, all force him to testify against himself. The dilemma drives him out of his mind, and before long he sees in a dream his *alter ego*, his Devil, and the two argue at length the pros and cons of his "unbounded resolution," which is to say, the pros and cons of whether God-and-immortality exist or do not exist.

Dostoevsky uses the device of the Devil as the voice of Ivan's rational principles in order to dramatize the nature and extent of Ivan's spiritual crisis. Ivan's confrontation with the Devil once again centers on the question of immortality, which is also the subject of the Legend of the Grand Inquisitor, and indeed the subject of the whole novel. The argument is the same as the argument of the Grand Inquisitor, in that both deny the existence of immortality. Ivan begins to perceive that his belief that there is no God-and-immortality is precisely the belief that the Devil preaches. "I maintain," says Ivan's Devil, "that nothing need be destroyed, that we only need to destroy the idea of God in man, that's how we have set to work. It's that we must begin with." "Since there is anyway no God and no immortality," says the Devil, "the new man may well become the man-god, even if he is the only one in the whole world, and, promoted to his new position, he may lightheartedly overstep all the barriers of the old morality of the old slave-man, if necessary. There is no law for God. Where God stands, the place is holy. Where I stand will be at once the foremost place . . . 'all things are lawful' and that's the end of it!"

The practical application of the Devil's philosophy is aired as Ivan subsequently relates his nightmare to Alyosha. Ivan sums up the Devil's argument as it applies to him as follows: " 'You are going to perform an act of heroic virtue and you don't believe in virtue, that's what tortures you and makes you angry, and that's why you are so vindictive.' He said that to me, Alyosha, and he knows what he says." Nonetheless the Devil believes that Ivan will testify despite the logic of not testifying, though he thinks that he will do so "in order to be praised," i.e., for unbelieving or "impure" motives; but Ivan denies the Devil's accusation. Alyosha, speaking for Dostoevsky, analyzes the state of Ivan's soul at this point: " 'God, in-Whom he disbelieves, and His truth were gaining mastery over his heart, which still refused to submit. . . .

Yes, if Smerdyakov is dead, no one will believe Ivan's evidence, but he will go and give it." Alyosha smiled softly, 'God will conquer.' " But in allowing God to conquer his heart, Ivan will, Alyosha predicts, do one of two things: "He will either rise up in the light of truth, or . . . he'll perish in hate, revenging on himself and on everyone his having served the cause he does not believe in [i.e., atheism]."

The overrriding reason that Dostoevsky has Smerdyakov kill himself is to give Ivan the opportunity to perform an act of perfect faith, precisely as Svidrigailov in *Crime and Punishment* must kill himself in order to permit Raskolnikov to confess, and thus to perform an act of perfect faith; for now that there is no one else to take the guilt except Ivan himself, then either he takes the blame alone or no one takes the blame, even though Ivan knows that no one will believe him. The question is, What will be the precise motive that impells Ivan at the trial to confess his part in the murder, and the answer is that he acts on the purest of possible motives, namely out of a genuine new-found belief in God-and-immortality. The man who had been fighting belief ever since he reached the age of reason, and whose reason was so powerful that he could argue against belief perhaps better than anyone else, is also the man whose reason was able to transcend the reason of the leading atheist intellectuals of his time or before his time, and thus enable him to confess his role, however inadvertent, in the death of his father, when there was no earthly reason to confess.

One can come to a full understanding of the nature of Ivan's spiritual struggles only if one has a full understanding of the power of Ivan's arguments against God-and-immortality, arguments which are perhaps more devastatingly convincing than those of the Enlighteners, or of the leading 19th-century atheist intellectuals. His rationale for the atheistic position is most effectively expressed in the famous Legend of the Grand Inquisitor, which I should like here to examine.

Like the article on Church jurisdiction, the Legend of the Grand Inquisitor is another example of how Ivan "diverts himself in his despair," as Father Zossima put it. The Legend of the Grand Inquisitor is a profoundly ironic document because it proposes a world of perfect unbelief even while the Grand Inquisitor himself recognizes the impossibility of living in a world of perfect unbelief. In both of these documents Ivan is simply exploring the logical consequences of belief and unbelief, with which the entire novel is preoccupied. Ivan's Legend of the Grand Inquisitor and the Life and Teachings of Father Zossima provide merely a formal and extended discussion of this most fundamental of all philosophical and theological questions.

The Legend in its literal meaning can no more be taken as a reflection of Ivan's atheism than it can of Dostoevsky's. For to take it at its face value, as even some notable Dostoevsky scholars have done, is to gloriously misrepresent the spirit of the entire novel. Unfortunately, no one is more likely to misinterpret the spirit of the novel than the reader who reads the Legend out of context, as many do who encounter it only in anthologies without context-restoring editorial commentary, or worse yet, with the commentary of editors who themselves do not perceive the irony of it, and who in fact sometimes mistake the Grand Inquisitor's atheistic proposal for Dostoevsky's own beliefs.

One has first of all to observe the importance of the prelude which leads to the Grand Inquisitor Legend. Ivan and Alyosha are sitting at a table in a tavern, and Ivan asks, "Why have we met here? To talk of my love for Katerina Ivanovna, of the old man and Dmitri? Of foreign travel? Of the fatal position of Russia? Of the Emperor Napoleon? Is that it?" It turns out that what they have met for, at Ivan's invitation, is to discuss "the eternal questions," and more specifically to enable the unbeliever, Ivan, to convey to the believer, Alyosha, his terrifying understanding of the consequences of unbelief, including his own. It is the communication to Alyosha of this understanding that constitutes what he calls his "confession," the confession of an uncomfortable atheist and unbeliever who wants to believe because his massive intellect cannot endure the condition of unbelief. The Legend itself must be understood as part of that confession.

And what are the eternal questions? They are, as Ivan observes, "the existence of God and immortality," or, among those who do not believe in God, it is "socialism," which, he says, is the same question turned inside out, i.e., the utopia on earth sought by unbelievers as opposed to the utopia in heaven sought by believers.

"Why have you been looking at me in expectation for the last three months?" asks Ivan. "To ask me what do you believe, or don't you believe at all? That's what your eyes have been meaning for these three months, haven't they?" And Alyosha replies, "Perhaps so." "Well, tell me where to begin," says Ivan, "give your orders. The existence of God, eh?"

Ivan begins with the revelation that he believes in God after all, despite his solemn denial before Alyosha and his father on the previous day. But his confession of faith does not approach even that of a deist, for he rejects God as fully as any atheist because he says that what he cannot accept is God's world. And yet, one cannot accept God without accepting God's world; Ivan knows it, just as Dostoevsky knows it.

God's world for Ivan is chiefly a theater for innocent suffering, and a terrible indictment of many of God's human creatures, whose artistic cruelty, especially to children, is above all a reflection on God. He therefore proceeds to regale Alyosha with a series of choice atrocities committed on children because in their case what he means is "so unmistakably clear." These include the soldierly practice of blowing a laughing baby's brains out with a pistol at close range and catching babies on the points of bayonets before their mothers' eyes. They include also the guillotining of Richard by the Christians after he had been converted to Christianity, or as Ivan put it, "they chopped off his head in brotherly fashion because he had found grace." They include the story of the father who unmercifully beat his seven-year-old daughter to the point of death and to the rhythm of its pitiful screams, "Daddy! Daddy!" They include further the five-year-old girl whose cultivated parents practiced all manner of refined cruelty on her, including smearing her face and filling her mouth with excrement by the mother, who slept well at night despite the child's groans. And they include, finally, the story of the eight-year-old boy who threw a stone that inadvertently wounded the paw of a dog belonging to a general, who thereupon called out to the boy's mother to watch the spectacle of her son being torn to pieces by a pack of hounds.

Ivan called up these stirring studies in sadism, (which Dostoevsky gleaned from newspapers) not only to reassure himself in his own faithlessness, but also to seek comfort by shaking the faith of Alyosha. For if Alyosha cannot help him in his search for faith, he will, out of

spite, try to make Alyosha lose his own. Ivan's objection
to God's world is that these examples of guiltless suffering surpass the understanding of his Euclidian mind,
which requires justice and punishment for offenders carried out "here on earth, and that I could see myself" and
not in "some remote infinite time and space." The prospect that a "higher harmony" is working itself out even in
the face of all the innocent suffering in the world will not
satisfy his belief in a world of unavenged tears.

While Ivan is relating these stories we witness one of
the finest displays of righteous indignation in all
literature. The irony is that this righteous indignation
loses much of its meaning except in a religious context,
for if these babies were not creatures with immortal
souls, created in the image of God, then there is not
much more reason to be horrified at the deaths of these
babies than there is of drowning kittens and puppies.
Furthermore, in a Godless world, guilty but unpunished
killers may go on enjoying life as surely as their victims
suffer death. In such instances there is either divine
justice or there is no justice at all, and Ivan, in crying out
for justice, denies the only kind of justice possible in the
cases that so outraged him. Alyosha, on the other hand,
being a believer, is vastly more justified in his righteous
indignation than Ivan, for to him these young victims are
creatures of God with immortal souls. Therefore such
crimes are not committed merely against men, but
against God. Alyosha perceives that murderers destroy
far more than Ivan perceives that they destroy. Alyosha
understands human life to be so sacred that, as he tells
Ivan, he would not sacrifice even the life of a single baby
in return for the earthly happiness of the rest of mankind.

Ivan had asked Alyosha whether there was anyone in
the world who would dare forgive the perpetrators of

these horrors, and Alyosha's answer is that "You have forgotten Him, and on Him is built the edifice, and it is to Him that they cry aloud, 'Thou art just, O Lord, for thy ways are revealed!' " Alyosha is in effect saying that Christ as God can indeed forgive all men and in fact died for them. He is that person who was tortured and killed in order that men might in the end find happiness and peace and rest.

Alyosha's answer, which is Christ's answer and Father Zossima's answer and Dostoevsky's answer, must now itself be answered, and if Ivan can answer it he will have struck a telling blow for atheism. And so, in the form of the Legend of the Grand Inquisitor, Ivan launches into what Dostoevsky himself says is a more powerful denial of God than his atheist enemies can even conceive. It is a tribute to Dostoevsky's genius as a believer that he can make out a vastly better case for atheism than the most belligerent and eloquent atheists in his or perhaps any other time, and that in a magnificent exercise in irony he should simultaneously be able to reduce the argument to an absurdity.

In examining these arguments and in emphasizing the irony of the Legend itself, it may be useful to consider here that there appear to be four possible conditions of man: (1) he may be by nature sinless and have an immortal soul; (2) he may be by nature sinless and not have an immortal soul; (3) he may be sinful and yet have an immortal soul; and (4) he may be sinful and not have an immortal soul. The validity of these categories depends, of course, a good deal upon the recognition that the word "sin" is strictly speaking a purely theological term, so that the atheist might substitute some such word as 'evil' or 'anti-social', or else use the term 'sin' figuratively.

The most desirable of these conditions no doubt is that man is sinless and has an immortal soul, a condition which would make him like God Himself, or at least like man in his prelapsarian state. But this position appears to be the farthest removed from reality, and no character in *The Brothers Karamazov* takes that position, though it is the position of some Romantic philosophers. The only place where Dostoevsky represents this position is his description of prelapsarian man in his *Dream of a Ridiculous Man*, and then only to show that men deserve much compassion for having lost paradise.

The notion that man is sinless and does not have an immortal soul is a position that, as we have seen, Dostoevsky fought against with all his energies because he found both premises totally unacceptable, despite the fact that it is the fundamental position of the Russian radicals and what Dostoevsky called the "socialists." He is so contemptuous of this view of man that he does not even regard it as a viable alternative in *The Brothers Karamazov*, and hence assigns it to his most contemptible characters, most notably Rakitin.

The third position, namely that man is a sinner with an immortal soul is the religious position in general, the Christian position in particular, and hence the position of Father Zossima and the other monks, of Alyosha, of Dmitri, and of Dostoevsky himself. It is the position that Dostoevsky had defended with all his mind and art during the last fifteen years or so of his life as not only the true position but ultimately the only workable position.

The fourth position, that man has no immortal soul but nonetheless is strongly disposed to wickedness is the most intolerable position and the most despairing, but it is the position of the most sophisticated atheistic intellec-

tuals of the present time, notably the atheist existentialists. This is the position also of Ivan and of the Grand
Inquisitor, who is Ivan in disguise. Dostoevsky himself
considers that the idea that men are soulless instruments
of evil is a position that must be dealt with seriously, so
seriously in fact that as he himself said, he wrote the entire novel to refute the argument of the Grand Inquisitor.

The Grand Inquisitor's insistence upon the weakness
of human nature is apparent at every turn. He calls men
"weak, vicious, worthless, and rebellious" and in various
places refers to them as "feeble" and "vile." In fact his
whole argument against Christ proceeds from the idea
that "man is weaker and baser by nature than Thou hast
believed him."

As the scene of the Legend opens, it is true that "the
people" have flocked around the returned Christ. They
are "irresistibly drawn to Him, they surround Him, they
flock about Him, follow Him," but that is because they
look upon Him not as their Savior, but as the healer of
their sick, and so long as He makes blind men see and
raises seven-year-old girls from the dead, they will indeed
follow Him. But they are also easily intimidated. When
the Grand Inquisitor observes his arch-enemy, Christ,
performing these miracles, he orders Him to be seized
and imprisoned. The "crowd" thereupon, in the
feebleness of its nature, is "cowed into submission and
trembling obedience," and "bows down to the earth like
one man, before the Old Inquisitor." That night when
the Inquisitor visits Christ in prison, to inform Him that
he will condemn Him and burn Him at the stake the next
day as the worst of heretics, he predicts that "the very
people who have kissed Thy feet, tomorrow at the
faintest sign from me will rush to heap up the embers on

Thy fire." And we are to understand that in their spiritual feebleness they will indeed.

Why does the Grand Inquisitor call Christ the "worst of heretics," and hence order that He be burned at the stake? The essence of the difference in their positions is that Christ has reaffirmed the immortality of men's souls and thus has insisted upon their essential humanness, a priceless gift, which, however, necessarily carries with it the burdens of freedom to choose between good and evil, and hence vast suffering on account of their natural disposition to choose evil. When Satan tempted Christ he tempted Him above all to give up man's immortality and his freedom, which is to say his humanness, in exchange for comfort and security and the happiness of mankind on earth, so that man could, to speak ironically, be elevated to the level of the beasts. All the Grand Inquisitor would ask of Christ is that men be allowed to live like happy beasts, and, in the end, die like happy beasts, which would inevitably include substituting a beast ethic for a human ethic; for when a man dies the grass grows over his grave and that is an end to him and it matters not at all what good or evil he did or what good or evil was done to him. But Christ would not succumb because as He said, "Man does not live by bread alone." If He had succumbed, then God-and-immortality would have no meaning and Christ Himself would have no meaning, as Christ well knew.

But the Grand Inquisitor insists that the gift of man's immortal soul and freedom, and hence his humanness, is too great a price to pay because it brings unbearable suffering to almost all men. Not only has Christ's decision led to "unrest, confusion, and unhappiness," but "millions of God's creatures have been created as a mockery" because they are too weak to benefit from their gift of freedom, and in fact suffer unbearably on account of it. "How are the weak ones to blame, because they could not endure what the strong have endured? How is the weak soul to blame that it is unable to receive such terrible gifts? Canst Thou have simply come to the elect for the elect?" Thus the Grand Inquisitor accuses Christ of resisting Satan's temptation and of insisting instead upon man's freedom, of "rejecting the only way by which men might be made happy"; for "nothing is more insupportable for a man and a human society than freedom." Therefore men do not seek the burden of freedom of the will and hence humanness and immortality. Given the choice of freedom or bread (i.e., between the possibility of goodness and the certainty of comfort), men will choose bread. "Thou didst promise the bread of Heaven," says the Grand Inquisitor, "but can it compare with the earthly bread in the eyes of the weak, ever sinful and ignoble race of men? And if for the sake of the bread of Heaven those thousands and tens of thousands shall follow Thee, what is to become of the millions and tens of thousands of millions of creatures who will not have the strength to forego the earthly bread for the sake of the heavenly?" Christ, then, is willing to sacrifice every vestige of happiness and security in the world for the sake of preserving the immortality of men's souls, and the prospect of Paradise, at least for some, because therein lies man's God-like nature, and hence his dignity.

If Christ had succumbed to Satan's temptations to provide all men with bread, i.e., comfort and peace and security in this world at the expense of life in the next, Christ would have taken away the distinction between men and beasts, and men would have become beasts, as both Christ and Satan knew—and not merely beasts but bad beasts. Satan, in turn, would have become lord of all the beasts since there would be nothing on earth but beasts and that is what the Grand Inquisitor advocates. The Grand Inquisitor's arguments are thus themselves Satanic and the Grand Inquisitor becomes the Devil's advocate, or more precisely a Devil-worshipper.

What the Grand Inquisitor proposes is that men be relieved of the "terrible gift" of freedom by rejecting the heavenly bread in favor of the earthly bread. Thus, those who hold absolute earthly authority also hold the bread and the conscience of the people in their hands and can thereby bring about one universal state and universal peace, "one unanimous and harmonious ant-heap." This is precisely what Christ could have brought about if only He had succumbed to the counsel of "the mighty spirit" Satan, and had relinquished the burden of men's immortal souls.

Once absolute earthly authority is established by benevolent dictators, the Grand Inquisitor sketches out his earthly paradise based not only upon the inescapable premise of the weak nature of men but upon what in their weakness they want or think they want:

> Then we shall give them the quiet humble happiness of weak creatures such as they are by nature. Oh, we shall persuade them at last not to be proud, for Thou didst lift them up and thereby taught them to be proud. We shall show them that they are weak, that they are only pitiful children, but that childlike happiness is the sweetest of all. They will become timid and will look to us and huddle close to us in fear, as chicks to the hen. They will marvel at us and will be awestricken before us, and will be proud at our being so powerful and clever, that we have been able to subdue such a turbulent flock of thousands of millions. They will tremble impotently before our wrath, their minds will grow fearful, they will be quick to shed tears like women and children, but they will be just as ready at a

sign from us to laughter and rejoicing, to happy mirth and
children's song. Yes, we shall set them to work, but in their
leisure hours we shall make their life like a child's game,
with children's songs and innocent dance. Oh, we shall
allow them even sin, they are weak and helpless, and they
will love us like children because we allow them to sin. We
shall tell them that every sin is expiated, if it is done with
our permission, that we allow them to sin because we love
them, and the punishment for these sins we take upon
ourselves. And we shall take it upon ourselves, and they
will adore us as their saviors who have taken on themselves
their sins before God. . . . And all will be happy, all the
millions of creatures except the hundred thousand who
rule over them. For only we, we who guard the mystery,
shall be unhappy. There will be thousands of millions of
happy babes, and a hundred thousand sufferers who will
have taken upon themselves the curse of the knowledge of
good and evil.

Such then is the Grand Inquisitor's utopia. It isn't
much of a utopia, but given the weak condition of
natural man in an atheistic world it is about the best that
can realistically be hoped for. It is a far more realistic
utopia than that of the typical 19th-century utopians
who based their plans on the notion of the natural
goodness of man instead of recognizing the natural
weakness of man. It may in fact be the first utopia before
the 20th century which proceeds upon the recognition of
man's natural disposition to evil. It is a utopia which
Dostoevsky, with his jaundiced view of Roman Cathol-
icism, felt the Catholic Church was already achieving.

But a sacrifice must be exacted in return for this
earthly semi-paradise, namely the taking away of men's
freedom, which is to say their humanness, which is to say
their immortal souls. "Peacefully they will die," says the
Grand Inquisitor, "peacefully they will expire in Thy
name, and beyond the grave they will find nothing but
death." But, he goes on, "we shall keep the secret [i.e.,

that there is no God-and-immortality], and for their happiness we shall allure them with the reward of heaven
and eternity, though if there were anything in the other
world, it certainly would not be for such as they."

However, not only must men give up their immortal
souls in order to achieve this measure of happiness and
security and comfort, but those who bring it about must
choose to abandon Christ and follow Satan. The Grand
Inquisitor tells Christ that "we have rejected Thee and
followed him [i.e., Satan]. We are not working with
Thee, but with *him*," for it is only Satan who can fulfill
the dreams of the millions upon millions of those who are
too weak to follow Christ and who would gladly sacrifice
their immortal souls and hence their freedom and
humanity for a few happy years on earth.

Yet the more eloquent and more appealing the Grand
Inquisitor's case against Christ becomes, the more fully
he feels the falseness of it. It is, in fact, a *reductio ad ab-
surdum* of the most persuasive case that can be made for
atheism, and the Grand Inquisitor (i.e., Ivan) is quite
aware of it.

While listening to Ivan relate the Legend, Alyosha
detects the Inquisitor's "secret," namely that "he does not
believe in God." The Inquisitor has placed himself in the
intolerable position of knowing that men are by nature
corrupt, and at the same time of denying God-and-
immortality. Alyosha knows it is an intolerable position,
which is why he exclaims: "But . . . that's absurd . . .
your poem is in praise of Jesus, not in blame of Him—as
you meant it to be." Alyosha recognizes that since men
are in such a plight only Christ can save them. Thus it is
Adam whom the Grand Inquisitor should be accusing,
for it is he who brought death and corruption to man,
whereas Christ brings life and salvation. How, then, is

man going to be good without God? The Grand Inquisitor offers the only possible alternative, namely a totalitarian utopia, in which men's freedom, and therefore their humanity, are taken from them in favor of child-like submission, a utopia in which the only kind of happiness is a beastlike happiness.

If Ivan was outraged by the atrocities perpetrated upon children by men made in God's image, he is secretly even more outraged by the idea that men are not made in God's image, which is what the Grand Inquisitor offers. In short, Ivan recognizes that the hell on earth which Christ has permitted is not as bad as the hell on earth that the Grand Inquisitor proposes, and yet he still cannot believe in Christ. This is the source of his spiritual agony. Christ never promised anyone a heaven on earth. He promised much suffering along with a little joy on earth and the possibility of true happiness in another world.

No one comprehends the agony of the Grand Inquisitor more fully than Christ Himself, and that is why Christ "approached the old man in silence and softly kissed him on his bloodless lips." Christ kissed the Grand Inquisitor not as a sign of his forgiveness, as is sometimes supposed, but for the same reason that Father Zossima kissed Dmitri in the monastery cell, i.e., out of recognition of his great spiritual suffering: the Grand Inquisitor because he sees the necessity of believing but still cannot believe, and Dmitri because he is a sinning believer and is going to believe more heartily and sin more heartily as his history proceeds. Similarly, when Alyosha kisses Ivan on the lips at the conclusion of the Legend, he does so out of the same recognition of Ivan's spiritual suffering, which is the same as the Grand Inquisitor's because Ivan is the Grand Inquisitor. Ivan acknowledges Alyosha's kiss as an echo of Christ's kiss with the words, "That's plagiarism. You stole that from my poem."

So, far from triumphing over Christ, the Grand Inquisitor is defeated by Christ, or rather by his recognition of the untenability of his own arguments. The Grand Inquisitor had spoken of the "miracle" of Satan putting the three questions to Christ and that Satan is "the wise and mighty spirit of the wilderness," as if the three temptations get at the heart of the weakness of Christ and the strength of Satan, whereas the Grand Inquisitor knows in his heart that Christ's resisting the temptations reflects the strength of Christ and the weakness of Satan. Thus, as Christ kisses the Grand Inquisitor, the Inquisitor knows that Christ is right and that he is wrong.

Christ is not allowed to reply to the Grand Inquisitor because, as the Grand Inquisitor says, "Thou hast no right to add anything to what Thou hast said of old," as if the Scriptures needed to be amended in the light of the Grand Inquisitor's or the Catholic Church's greater understanding, or as if Christ's teachings need to be "corrected." In his tortured condition of unbelief, the Grand Inquisitor might well wish that Christ had spoken, though he says that "I know too well what Thou wouldst have said." What indeed would Christ have said? Christ would have said what Dostoevsky has been saying all along, namely that men in all their weakness cannot live without Him and still maintain their dignity. All that is really needed is Christ's kiss, and as Dostoevsky says, "that was all His answer." Thus the incredible verbal eloquence of the Grand Inquisitor is vanquished by the even more incredible eloquence of Christ's silence.

"The kiss glows in his heart, but the old man adheres to his idea." Thus Ivan sums up the Grand Inquisitor's dilemma, which is to say his own dilemma, of perceiving the necessity of believing but not being able to believe.

As we have seen, Ivan later in the novel is again confronted by the Satanic argument against Christ, this time by Satan himself in a dream. But whereas after the Grand Inquisitor episode Ivan walked away and was merely "overcome by insufferable depression," after his encounter with Satan himself, and after hearing the same arguments over again, only in a different form and a different context, he becomes more than depressed; he goes mad. And the reason that he goes mad is that in the interval he has not merely seen but felt the logical consequences of atheism, namely the murder of his own father, a murder carried out in the name of atheism. Having previously talked himself into unbelief by his reason, he appears in the end to be beginning to scare himself into belief by his understanding.

CHAPTER V

THE KARAMAZOVS AND
THE PROBLEM OF GOODNESS

Dostoevsky was concerned in *The Brothers Karamazov* to demonstrate that atheism can provide philosophical support for crimes such as Smerdyakov's killing Old Karamazov and for vices such as those which Old Karamazov himself specialized in. The idea is that since there is no punishment in the next life for evil deeds committed in this life, then "evil" deeds are permissible whenever they appear to be to one's advantage. Without the influence of religion, Dostoevsky insists, or at least a religious heritage, men in their natural state are so strongly inclined to commit such deeds that they will end in destroying not only themselves but others as well.

But Dostoevsky is quite as much interested in demonstrating that if there is no immortality there is often no adequate reason to perform good deeds either, especially deeds that cause the kind of sacrifice and pain that must be continually endured in order to keep civilization from unravelling. Thus Ivan's conclusion that "If there is no immortality there is no virtue and everything is lawful" works two ways: there is not only no logical reason for "clever" men not to perform pleasurable bad deeds, but there is no logical reason for "clever" men to perform painful good deeds. If there is no immortality then the only logical ethic is a beast ethic and there is no more reason for clever men to sacrifice their interests than there is for a cat to sacrifice its interests. Therefore, atheists who pursue a truly human ethic, i.e., who in any way sacrifice their own interests for the sake of others are, as Rakitin insisted, "fools."

And yet men do persist in making moral decisions which work against their earthly advantage, or at least their earthly pleasures, and *The Brothers Karamazov* contains descriptions of a good many of them. One of the prime examples of such behavior, as we have seen, is Dmitri's monumental feat of restraint in not violating the virtue of the delicious Katerina even when he was in a state of high heat and when he could have done so with complete impunity. Instead, he left her virtue intact and still gave her the money she needed to save her father from ruin. Another is Dmitri's disastrous efforts to return to Katerina the 3,000 rubles which he had lavished on Grushenka and which caused him to end up in a Siberian prison camp, even though he knew that she was willing to forgive the deed and forget the rubles. Still another is Ivan's decision to confess his part in the murder of his father, even though there was no earthly reason to confess.

In such major actions by such major characters, Dostoevsky had in mind to demonstrate that men do not live by bread alone, and to suggest that if there is no God-and-immortality then Dmitri and Ivan have acted like utter fools and we are fools ourselves for admiring such actions. It is incidents like these which help Dostoevsky refute the Grand Inquisitor, who argues that men are better off in an atheistic world ruled by a benevolent despotism created in exchange for men's immortal souls, and hence their freedom and dignity.

There are a number of other major episodes in *The Brothers Karamazov* that are difficult to fit into the plot of the novel unless one understands that Dostoevsky uses them precisely to demonstrate that if there is no God-and-immortality, then self-sacrificing good deeds have no meaning and are in fact monumentally illogical. I should like in this chapter to consider some of these episodes.

Among them are certain events in the life of Father Zossima. Father Zossima's conversion to Christianity and his desire to enter the monastery grew out of a quarrel with his rival-in-love, which led to a duel that the young Zossima provoked by insulting him in the presence of a large company. On the night before the duel was to take place he returned home in a foul humor and beat his servant more mercilessly than ever before. Then suddenly, he says, "something happened that in very truth was the turning-point of my life." He could not sleep that night because he was greatly disturbed that he should have beaten "a fellow-creature made in the likeness and image of God." He began to experience a spiritual transformation, which actually had its origin in his religious training at home, but on that night he recalled his brother Markel's dying words, that all are responsible for all, and he thereupon came to some decisions that changed the course of his life. The realization that men are God's creatures and that thus all are responsible for all in effect led him to the revelation that men do not live by bread alone after all, that the *summum bonum* of life is not comfort and security and pleasure but goodness and sacrificial love and, inescapably, suffering.

The force of Zossima's conversion is underscored when he thereupon jumps into his comrade's carriage and sets off for the duel with words, "Have you ever

seen a conqueror? Here is one before you." His friend
takes this remark to mean that he is boasting that he is
going to win the duel, and so he replies, "Well, brother,
you'll keep up the honor of the uniform I can see." But
the reader knows that what Zossima meant is that what
he had conquered was his desire to live by bread alone,
i.e., that he had conquered his desire to live only by
desire. He had demonstrated it once by bowing down to
his servant and in full uniform asking his forgiveness with
such abjectness that his servant was perplexed to the
point that he asked of his master, "Am I worth it?" And
he went on to demonstrate it again by refusing to fire his
shot in the duel. It would have been much easier and far
more to his earthly advantage to have gone through with
the duel, because he was not afraid, and because he
would have thus preserved not only his own honor but
also the honor of his regiment. Furthermore, his opponent had fired first and merely grazed his head, so that it
would have been particularly easy to fire his own shot,
thereby winning not only the duel but perhaps even the
hand of the lady he loved, who was by then his
opponent's wife. In short, the earthly rewards for carrying the duel forward might have been very great. Instead,
he declined to fire his shot and as a result was obliged to
endure all manner of ridicule and revilement. "He has
disgraced the uniform," some said. When he tried to explain why he did not fire, and how he came to realize that
all are responsible for all, and when he stated his resolve
to enter the monastery after his revelation about the need
to love God's creatures, his comrades laughed at him and
thought him mad. It is to be noted, however, that not
everyone laughed at him and thought him mad: his opponent accepted his decision as sincere and his opponent's
wife expressed her appreciation and gratitude, and

Zossima himself felt such peace of mind as he had never before experienced.

Thus Dostoevsky offers us a fairly clear-cut example of how a man may choose a spiritual advantage over an earthly advantage on the grounds that man is a spiritual creature; otherwise Zossima's actions are utter folly and he deserves all the ridicule and contempt which had been heaped upon him. What Dostoevsky is saying above all, not only in these episodes, but in the entire novel, is that the ultimate purpose of life is not comfort but goodness, but with the understanding that the purpose of life as goodness makes no sense unless God-and-immortality exist, and that comfort should be the end of life if God-and-immortality do not exist.

One of Dostoevsky's most compelling examples of this dialectic is the episode which followed after Zossima's refusal to fight the duel, in the form of the story of the "mysterious visitor." No one saw in Zossima's behavior so dramatic an act of faith as the "mysterious visitor," whose name we learn, in time, is Mikhail. "You are, I see, a man of great strength of character," says Mikhail, "as you have dared to serve the truth, even when by doing so you risked incurring the contempt of all." In fact, it is on account of Mikhail's perception of the young Zossima's great faith that he comes to him with his problem, a problem which, except perhaps for Ivan's story, may illustrate as well as any episode in any novel or perhaps anywhere in life the phenomenon that man does not live by bread alone and that unless there is God-and-immortality there is no adequate reason not to live by bread alone. Mikhail's problem, which he proceeds to reveal to Zossima, is that he has committed a horrible crime: he has killed a woman, a widow, whom he loved but who in turn loved another, and he contrived the murder so that the suspicion would fall on a servant, who was subsequently tried and convicted but who died before he was sentenced. At first the mysterious visitor felt no pangs of conscience, and in fact went on to marry a loving woman and had three loving children. But as time passed, the crime more and more preyed on his mind, and even though he tried to atone for it by turning philanthropist, the more he was respected the more intolerable the guilt became until he reached the point that he wanted to confess the crime publicly and take the consequences; and he has come to Zossima, to this young man of spectacular religious faith, for advice as to what he should do.

Thus Dostoevsky has provided the reader with a test *par excellence* of the meaning of belief in God-and-immortality. If man does indeed live by bread alone, like the beasts, there is no reason whatsoever for the visitor to confess his crime to Zossima or to anyone else. The crime is over and done with; it happened fourteen years ago; the mysterious visitor was not apprehended or even suspected by anyone; the person who was convicted of the crime died a natural death even before he began to serve his sentence. Furthermore, Mikhail had tried to atone for the crime by performing a multitude of good deeds; and if he were to confess the crime, not only would he himself be sent to Siberia, but, as he says, "My wife may die of grief" and his children would become a convict's children, and "what a memory of me I shall leave in their hearts."

Father Zossima's reply is the reply of the true believer: "Go. Confess. Everything passes, only the truth remains." Mikhail does not want to hear from young Zossima what he knows that he will hear. "But need I?" he exclaims, "Must I? No one has been condemned, no one has been sent to Siberia in my place, the man died of a fever. And I've been punished by my sufferings for the blood I shed. And I shan't be believed, they won't believe my proofs. Need I confess, need I? I am ready to go on suffering all my life for the blood I have shed, if only my wife and children may be spared. Will it be just to ruin them with me? Aren't we making a mistake? What is right in this case? And will people recognize it, will they appreciate it, will they respect it?"

Once again he asks, "Decide my fate," and once again Zossima, with all the understanding and all the compassion of a saint, repeats the words, "Go and confess." "All will understand your sacrifice," he tells him, "if not at once they will alter; for you have served the truth, the higher truth, not of the earth." As authority for his counsel, Zossima quotes two passages from the Bible: the first is a passage in *John*, which also serves as the epigraph of the novel, and which with the greatest possible significance verifies the immortality of the soul: "Verily, verily I say unto you, except a corn of wheat fall into the ground and die, it abideth alone, but if it die, it bringeth forth much fruit." And the other is from *Hebrews*, which also affirms the fact and possible consequences of the immortality of the soul: "It is a fearful thing to fall into the hands of the living God."

Mikhail is horrified by the appropriateness of the passages and wonders whether they can have been written by man, to which Zossima replies, "The Holy Spirit wrote them," thus reaffirming that the Scriptures are revelation, not mere philosophy, or history, or poetry. Mikhail, trembling all over, now accepts Zossima's advice, saying, "So I have been for fourteen years 'in the hands of the living God', that's how one must think of these fourteen years. Tomorrow I will beseech those hands to let me go." And so he departs resolved to confess his crime, which he does the next day at his own birthday party, to which he had invited the whole town.

The point of this episode is that Zossima's advice stems from a perfect faith. For all his compassion for Mikhail he did not hesitate before advising him to give himself up, despite the fact that he too was to suffer, as he knew he would, from having given it; for nothing came of the stranger's confession because the case was dismissed for insufficient evidence. The stranger himself was judged to be insane, and he in fact died within a week of the confession. As a result, the townspeople began to suspect Zossima of evil influence upon Mikhail; and Mikhail's wife, as well as the whole town, blamed him for Mikhail's death and criticized him, though soon after, Zossima entered the monastery without having told anyone what had happened and with utter conviction that his advice was right. Thus the episode about "the mysterious stranger" is really more about Zossima than about Mikhail because it was at least as hard for Zossima to say "go and confess," as it was for Mikhail actually to go and confess.

Unlike the young Zossima, Mikhail's faith was something less than perfect to the extent that he visited Zossima once again with the intention of killing him because Zossima knew the truth not only about Mikhail but the truth about what Mikhail should do, and Mikhail hated him for it. "Let me tell you," he later tells Zossima, "you were never nearer death." But he did not kill him for approximately the same reason that Dmitri did not kill his father. "The Lord," explained Mikhail, "vanquished the devil in my heart." Ultimately the Lord also caused him to confess his crime, and on his deathbed he felt a peace he had never known before.

The big question that the story of Mikhail raises is, what does the reader think of it all, for the episode was designed to test the reader's faith quite as much as it was Zossima's and Mikhail's. The reaction of the logical atheist should be that the confession was an act of utter stupidity and that furthermore Zossima himself was wholly wrong, not to say cruel, in counseling it, for if man does indeed live by bread alone, nothing could be more inconsistent with that premise than to be the cause or the victim of all that misery—and all for nothing. Even if the reader is a believer in any sort of impersonal or indifferent God, his reaction ought to be essentially the same as that of the atheist, since only the idea of a personal God and the idea of personal immortality, indeed of a heaven and a hell, can give any meaning to or justification for Zossima's advice or Mikhail's acting upon it. Perhaps most readers would understand and sympathize with Zossima and Mikhail's actions and admire them but would not themselves so easily counsel as Zossima counselled or comply as Mikhail complied. To that extent their faith is merely imperfect. Those who without qualm approve wholeheartedly Zossima's advice and Mikhail's confession come closest to a perfect faith.

Still another episode in *The Brothers Karamazov* which illustrates pointedly that men will not live by bread alone is the story of Captain Snegiryov. Snegiryov was an officer who had been "put to shame for his vices," and discharged from the army. He subsequently had "sunk into terrible destitution," even though he had a "litter," as he called it, of sick children as well as a wife who is not only sick but insane. In order to ward off starvation, Captain Snegiryov came into Old Karamazov's employ, and one of his dirty business assignments was to deliver to Grushenka some of Dmitri's IOUs with the idea that Grushenka should try to collect on them and in the process, as Old Karamazov planned it, to get his son thrown into prison and thus ruin him. Dmitri, recognizing the foulness of the deed, confronted Captain Snegiryov in the tavern and, in front of Snegiryov's sensitive son Ilyusha, pulled him out of the tavern by his thin red beard, his "wisp of tow," as it came to be called.

Everyone, including Dmitri, came to recognize how despicable this act was and how cruelly Captain Snegiryov was humiliated by it, particularly as his son had witnessed it. It was, as Katerina observed, "one of those actions of which only Dmitri Fyodorovich would be capable in his anger." "Father, dear father, how he insulted you," cried Ilyusha, as father and son sat trembling in each other's arms.

In getting at the meaning of Captain Snegiryov's story, the reader is to consider not only Snegiryov's humiliation but also his destitution. He is a good but wretched man living with his wretched family in a hovel, all of which Dostoevsky describes in painful detail; yet despite his wretchedness he still retains the honor and pride and dignity that all men are entitled to, provided that there is God-and-immortality after all. Therefore the scene is set so that we may observe Snegiryov's behavior when Alyosha, at the behest of Dmitri's fiancée, Katerina, offers 200 rubles to the captain "not by way of compensation to prevent him from taking proceedings . . . but simply a token of sympathy, of a desire to assist him."

When Alyosha offers Captain Snegiryov the 200 rubles, the reader witnesses one of Dostoevsky's most masterful psychological studies. The captain runs over in his mind all that he might do with this 200 rubles, which is, as he says, more money than he has seen in four years. It could, first of all, provide the means to carry out his and his son's dreams of buying a horse and cart and putting mamma and the girls inside, all bundled up, leaving the "horrid town" in which they lived and were so cruelly humiliated, and moving to some place where their past would not be known. He could also, he speculates, pay for the medicine and mineral water and baths that would cure his wife and his daughter Mina, who would no longer have to say "I am a useless cripple, no good to anyone." He could send his precocious daughter Varvara to Petersburg to continue her studies and to work for the emancipation of Russian women, and furthermore not only pay back to her the 16 rubles which she had previously brought back from Petersburg and which had to be used for living expenses, but also free her from the household and nursing duties that were crushing her. "You can't understand what these two hundred rubles mean to me now," he cried out to Alyosha in his ecstasy. "Now I can get a servant with the money . . . I can get medicine for the dear creatures, I can send my student to Petersburg, I can buy beef, I can feed them properly. Good Lord, but it's a dream."

We are indeed to understand that the money means everything to the captain and his family. Perhaps even their continued existence depends upon it, and not only is there more where that came from, but, as Alyosha says, "No one will know of it. It will give rise to no unjust slander." Thus Dostoevsky has made the arguments for taking the money overwhelming. If man lives by bread alone, Captain Snegiryov should seize the money as eagerly as a hungry dog who seizes upon a meaty bone thrown him by the butcher who had viciousy kicked him the previous day, but who then takes such pity on the dog that he offers him the best cuts of meat in his store, all he wants.

And yet the captain suddenly takes the two hundred ruble notes which he had been holding in his hand all the while, crumples them up savagely, throws them to the ground, tramples on them, and shouts, "So much for your money! So much for your money! So much for your money! So much for your money!" and runs off.

Evidently, then, Captain Snegiryov does not live by bread alone any more than the mysterious visitor, even when bread alone might have saved both him and his family. We are told three times that the captain did not know "till the very last moment" that he would fling the notes away, but in that moment, his God-like nature overcame his beast-like nature and that act itself constitutes a kind of proof of his divinity, as Dostoevsky would have it, a kind of intimation of immortality, because it would otherwise have been an act of utter madness to reject the rubles.

Alyosha dissects, with Dostoevskyian penetration, Captain Snegiryov's behavior by explaining to Katerina that the captain was mortified not only that he had betrayed to Alyosha his delight at the prospect of the 200 rubles, but that he had bared to Alyosha his innermost soul. He had for a time forgotten that he had been horribly humiliated, that he was an honorable man, and that he would not sell his honor.

These are all motives that would not have disturbed the beasts; but men are different from beasts, Dostoevsky tells us over and over again, not by virtue of their reason, for indeed the captain's reason made out an overwhelming case for taking the money, but by virtue of their spiritual nature, which, as Dostoevsky insists, has meaning only if there is God-and-immortality.

Alyosha in his analysis of Captain Snegiryov predicts that "tomorrow" when Alyosha offers the money to the captain again, he will take it; and we later learn that he did take it. Does this phenomenon mean then that the captain is like the beasts after all, and like them lives by bread alone? As Alyosha explains it, the captain can now take the money in good conscience because by refusing it the first time he had already demonstrated to himself adequately that he would not sell his honor. From an artistic point of view, however, there would appear to be another reason: since we are to understand that by not taking the money the captain would have "ruined himself," as Alyosha says, as well as his family, the prospect that the whole Snegiryov family would meet some dire end on account of Snegiryov's action becomes too painful for the reader to contemplate, just as the prospect of Mikhail, the mysterious visitor, spending long years in Siberia and of his family suffering infinitely on account of his confession is also too painful to contemplate. Thus, just as Mikhail dies and spares the reader the pain of his not dying, so Captain Snegiryov brings himself to accept the money and so saves both himself and his family. To this extent, then, theological principles give way to aesthetic principles. But Dostoevsky had nonetheless made his point, and devastatingly so.

There is some evidence to suggest that Smerdyakov in the end also had time to recognize that he himself does not live by bread alone and that "all is not lawful" after all. In Dostoevsky's later novels he always intends some philosophical significance from characters who commit suicide, including quite possibly Smerdyakov's. He may very well have been making the same point that he was making with Zossima's duel, with Mikhail's confession, and with Captain Snegiryov's refusing the 200 rubles. His story, more nearly, however, parallels Ivan's. The motive for Smerdyakov's suicide is not wholly clear, for, as Dostoevsky says, it was "impossible to tell whether it was remorse he was feeling or not," when he hanged himself. But there is much in the novel to suggest that even Smerdyakov—the supposedly comfortable atheist, who idealized the "clever" people who could successfully break God's laws on the grounds that there is no God—even he had come to recognize the impossibility of living by bread alone and that even he underwent a kind of spiritual conversion, or at least a spiritual reversal which led to suicide out of some sort of spiritual despair.

All the earlier exercises in spiritual cynicism that we get from Smerdyakov, including his rationale for killing Old Karamazov, his anecdote about the soldier who, in his view, rather than being martyred should have accepted a false religion (thus saving his life and spending the remainder of his days repenting), and his other philosophical musings suggest that he is as comfortable an atheist as Rakitin or Miusov. The notion that this cook, this lackey, this non-thinker who seems so comfortably set in his atheism with what he thinks is the full support of the brilliant Ivan, should undergo a spiritual reversal and should conclude on his own that perhaps there may be such a thing as virtue and therefore God-and-immortality after all, may come as something of a surprise. And yet there is a good deal of evidence that he did so. Perhaps the first hint comes from the conversation between Smerdyakov and Ivan just after Ivan learns, thunderstruck, that Smerdyakov murdered his father:

> "Do you know, I am afraid that you are a dream, a phantom sitting before me," Ivan muttered.

"There's no phantom here, but only us two and one other. No doubt he is here, that third, between us."

"Why is he? Who is here? What third person?" Ivan cried in alarm, looking about him, his eyes hastily searching in every corner.

"The third is God Himself, Providence. He is the third beside us now. Only don't look for Him, you won't find Him."

Smerdyakov might appear to be jesting in his reference to God's presence and one might be ready enough to pass it off as a piece of cynicism typical of Smerdyakov, but shortly thereafter Ivan discovers a book on the table which one would not expect Smerdyakov to be reading, a book entitled *The Sayings of the Holy Father Isaac the Syrian*. Dostoevsky makes nothing of the fact but merely notes it. More significant, however, is that Smerdyakov, having explained to the dumfounded Ivan all the details of how he murdered Old Karamazov, gives to Ivan the 3,000 rubles which he had stolen and which he had intended to use to begin "a new life" abroad. It is true that Ivan, in possession of this money, is thus able to offer it at the trial as feeble evidence of his and Smerdyakov's guilt. But Dostoevsky seems to suggest that Smerdyakov is indeed making some sort of sacrifice in giving it up. If he were to act in accordance with his former philosophy that man does indeed live by bread alone, there being no God, if he still recognized that "cleverness" is the supreme virtue, then he would without qualm have set off for Europe to start a new life. But he does not. The dialogue here is highly significant:

"And now, I suppose, you believe in God, since you are giving back the money?"

"No, I don't believe," whispered Smerdyakov.

"Then why are you giving it back?"

"Leave off . . . that's enough;" Smerdyakov waved his hand again.

"You used to say yourself that everything was lawful, so now why are you so upset too?"

That last word "too" suggests that Smerdyakov is now experiencing at least some spiritual qualms, and perhaps not qualms merely, but a full-scale struggle, a struggle which he in part loses by the fact of his suicide. He evidently now has some dim recognition that all is not lawful and that God may exist after all, despite his denials.

And finally, Smerdyakov's suicide note suggests some sort of sacrificial act based upon the uncertainty of his unbelief, especially since he knows perfectly well that Dmitri will be convicted, that no one will believe Ivan's story, and that he will himself therefore get off scot free—if he acts in accordance with his principle of "cleverness," based upon his atheistic premises. The note reads: "I destroyed my life of my own will and desire so as to throw no blame on any one." Both the note and the fact of Smerdyakov's suicide seem to be a clear violation of his professed principle that man lives by bread alone, the principle which caused him to kill Old Karamazov. Smerdyakov evidently found himself faced with two choices, either to go and confess with Ivan to having killed Old Karamazov or else be killed by Ivan. He could not bring himself to confess, either out of lack of courage or a sincere belief that Ivan, not he himself, was the real murderer, and yet he seems not to have wanted to make a murderer of Ivan. Since he was going to lose his life in any case, he chooses a way that would prevent Ivan from becoming a murderer.

Such an interpretation is not conclusive, but it is consistent with Dostoevsky's overall intention in the novel, and it perhaps serves better than any other to explain the incidents I have described. If so, then even Smerdyakov, who Ivan finally admitted was far more intelligent than he had previously supposed him to be, perceived a glimmer of the truth which struck Ivan with full fury. And yet in all this speculation it must not be forgotten that Smerdyakov's suicide is crucial to the novel because it enables Ivan to perform a perfect act of faith by confessing at the trial to having been responsible for the death of his father.

There seems little doubt but that Dostoevsky intended episodes such as I have discussed in this chapter as a refutation of the Enlighteners' and the nineteenth-century atheist intellectuals' insistence that reason can solve the world's problems better than religion. In each instance reason should have dictated that these characters, Zossima, Captain Snegiryov, the "mysterious visitor," and Smerdyakov, as well as Ivan and Dmitri, should have acted in a manner precisely the opposite of that in which they did act. In each instance they made a moral choice that was essentially super-rational, a choice based upon the premise that man is indeed a spiritual creature, that he by no means lives by bread alone. They made choices which would make no sense without the existence of God-and-immortality.

CHAPTER VI

HURRAH FOR KARAMAZOV!

Behind the lines of the battleground on which God and the Devil are struggling for the souls of Dmitri and Ivan, another spiritual conflict is taking place between Alyosha the believer and Rakitin the unbeliever. In the hands of a novelist less capable than Dostoevsky this conflict might constitute the entire war, but in *The Brothers Karamazov* it is more nearly a skirmish. Dmitri being the uncomfortable believer, and Ivan the uncomfortable unbeliever, the chief interest focuses on them on account of their suffering, portrayed in the grand Dostoevsky manner. Alyosha, depicted as the comfortable believer, except for one lapse, and Rakitin, depicted as the comfortable unbeliever, with no lapses, cannot be expected to provide the high drama of the professional sufferers in the novel, but the conflict between them adds much to its spiritual dimension.

Both Alyosha and Rakitin are young, both are novices in a monastery, and both are to leave the monastery. But there the similarity ends, for while Alyosha goes out into the world to preach the gospel of Christianity, Rakitin goes out to teach the gospel of atheism.

Rakitin's philosophical crime is that he is guilty of repudiating what Dostoevsky considered to be the two most fundamental premises about man's nature, namely that he is a sinner and that he has an immortal soul. In his imperception Rakitin readily ridicules Ivan's conclusion that "If there is no immortality, there is no virtue and everything is lawful," and substitutes instead his own theory, namely that "humanity will find in itself the power to live for virtue even without believing in immortality. It will find it in love for freedom, for equality, for fraternity." We get something of Dostoevsky's attitude toward Rakitin's doctrine from Dmitri, who has occasion to recall it to Alyosha when Alyosha visits him in prison: "Rakitin says one can love humanity without God," he observes. "Well, only a snivelling idiot can maintain that."

Whenever Dostoevsky portrays the ideas of incorrigible atheists, he makes their ideas all the more abhorrent by making those who hold them abhorrent. It was so with Pyotr Verhovensky, for example, in *The Possessed* and with Luzhin in *Crime and Punishment*, and it is so with Rakitin. In fact, he makes Rakitin himself the best refutation of Rakitin's own ideas, for not only is he not much given to loving humanity, but he comes close to living the life of the logical atheist like Old Karamazov, as opposed to the virtuous atheist like Ivan. In his own way he outdoes Old Karamazov himself, who as a logical atheist vows to go on "sinning to the end" because he is certain that there is no such thing as sin and that the end is really the end. But whereas Old Karamazov's sins are highly unoriginal, Rakitin makes "cleverness" the highest virtue, for he believes with Smerdyakov and the other logical atheists that "many people are honest because they are fools."

Rakitin is quite possibly the most despicable of all the rogues in Dostoevsky's grand gallery. We are told that Rakitin is "of an uneasy and envious temper," that he is "well aware of his own considerable abilities, and in his self-conceit he "nervously exaggerated them." He is also "particularly clever in getting around people and assuming whatever part thought most to their taste, if he detected the slightest advantage to himself for doing so." Ivan calls him "a liberal booby with no talents whatsoever." Dmitri says of him," he is a pig, a regular pig, but he's very arch, the rascal," and Alyosha, who is the least criticial of him observes that "he abuses everyone." And one of the surest signs that he is a scoundrel is that Madame Holakhov regards him as "a most religious and devout young man," or at least she does until she learns that he is indeed a scoundrel.

Dostoevsky shows us the logical atheist in action by showing how Rakitin in his spiritual imperception regularly miscalculates the motives of others and generally fails even while trying to exercise the logical atheist's virtue of cleverness. When, for example, Father Zossima bows down before Dmitri in the monastery cell, everyone is mystified by the gesture except Rakitin, who gloriously misreads the significance of it. "There's nothing wonderful about it," he tells Alyosha. "He predicted a crime and marked the criminal." He assures Alyosha that he has "suddenly understood your brother Dmitri, seen right into the very heart of him at once," and out of this powerful insight of the comfortable atheist he has been able to deduce that Dmitri will indeed kill his father. Thus Rakitin's estimate of Dmitri marks a telling contrast to that of Alyosha, who observes simply that "It won't come to that," and especially of Father Zossima, who did indeed "see right into the heart of him at once," and who thus bowed down to him with an understanding far beyond Rakitin's poor powers, namely out of recognition of the suffering Dmitri will endure on account of the peculiarly potent combination of honor and passion in his make-up.

Similarly Rakitin in all his smugness has no appreciation of the agony that Alyosha suffers when Father Zossima's corpse begins to decompose prematurely. Even Father Paissey cannot shield Alyosha from the shock of the phenomenon. On walking out of the monastery — a symbol of how badly his faith is shaken — the last person he wants to run into is Rakitin, knowing Rakitin as he does. But it is precisely Rakitin whom he does run into. When Rakitin observes that Alyosha's face has lost its "famous mildness," Alyosha utters almost the only harsh words we hear from him in the entire novel, "Let me alone." The cozy unbeliever begins to taunt the shattered believer. "Say, Alyosha, you have surprised me, do you hear?. . . . I always took you for an educated man. . . . Can you really be so upset simply because your old man has begun to stink? So now you are in a temper with your God, you are rebelling against Him. He hasn't given promotion. He hasn't bestowed the order of merit."

Alyosha is in fact so near despair at this moment that he rebels against God by proposing to break his fast with an orgy comprised of a banquet of sausage, vodka, and Grushenka. Rakitin is delighted to help him to all three — having already agreed for a fee of 25 rubles (and some champagne, too) to bring Alyosha to Grushenka so that she might, in the complexity of her emotions, seduce him. His mouth waters at the prospect of helping this falling angel to fall, perhaps as low as he himself has fallen.

Rakitin's callous, indeed vicious behavior towards Alyosha in his great grief is set off against the instinctive compassion of Grushenka when she learns that Alyosha's elder is dead. Even before this revelation she knew the difference between Rakitin, whom she calls "a toadstool" because he has no conscience, and Alyosha, whom she calls a "falcon," because he is *her* conscience, and, ironically, loves him for it, "with all my soul," she says, even though at the same time she hates him for his goodness. Upon learning of the death of Father Zossima, she "crosses herself devoutly," slips off Alyosha's lap and takes a place on the sofa exclaiming, "Goodness, what have I been doing, sitting on his knee like this at such a moment." Alyosha marks the difference between Rakitin's and Grushenka's reaction to his distress: "I've lost a treasure such as you have never had, and you cannot judge me now," he tells Rakitin. "You had much better look at her—do you see how she has pity on me? I came here to find a wicked soul—and I've found a true sister. I have found a treasure—a loving heart." By the time the scene ends, Rakitin accepts the 25 rubles in front of Alyosha, who comes away with his spirits in good part restored, thanks to Grushenka, and Rakitin goes away cursing them both.

And yet, for all his contempt for Alyosha and his spiritual troubles, Rakitin is still capable of the monumentally hypocritical, that is to say "clever," writing of a pamphlet on "The Life of the Deceased Elder, Father Zossima," which was "full of profound and religious reflections," and, more significantly, included "an excellent and devout dedication to the Bishop." This specimen of cleverness causes Dmitri at the trial to expose Rakitin as "an opportunist, who doesn't believe in God," but who "succeeded in taking the Bishop in." For the logical atheist, however, it is a grand example of the "virtue" of cleverness.

On the matter of Dmitri's innocence or guilt in the murder of his father, the contrast between Alyosha's and Rakitin's view is no less remarkable and no less consistent. Alyosha, as we have seen, knew "in his heart" that Dmitri was innocent, whereas Rakitin is so certain of his guilt that he writes an article explaining that Dmitri couldn't help killing his father, that he was a "victim of his environment." Actually, the conclusion is quite understandable. Rakitin in his imperception could hardly suppose that any "higher feeling," as Alyosha put it, could possibly take hold of Dmitri at the critical moment; and being a believer in the natural goodness of man, he quite logically concluded that Dmitri, like all murderers, must be a victim of his environment, for no man would kill another as an act of free will and in full possession of his senses. Thus, at the trial he regales the jury with all manner of noble social sentiments, attacking serfdom and the political disorder in Russia, with the philosophical implication that man will reform if society is reformed, rather than that society will reform (as Dostoevsky insists) if man reforms.

But Rakitin's exercises in atheistic cleverness lead, in time, to his disgrace. Having rebuked Dmitri for failing to exercise the virtue of cleverness by getting himself "into a mess, like a fool, for the sake of 3,000 rubles," Rakitin unfolds his own master plan in accordance with the doctrine of cleverness, namely to marry the good-hearted but weak-minded Madame Hohlakhov, to "collar" her 150,000 rubles, to buy a house in Petersburg, and bring out a newspaper "on the socialist side" to serve as an organ of atheism. And this he proposes to do by playing upon her sentimentality, her stupidity, and her vanity. "When I get hold of the silly woman's fortune, I can be of great social utility," he says, to which Dmitri observes with all the authority of Dostoevsky himself, "They have this social justification for every nasty thing they do."

The reader, Dostoevsky hopes, will take some satisfaction in the shame of Rakitin, whose ingratiating poem on Madame Hohlakhov's swollen foot, Perhotin, his rival in love, properly ridicules, and who is summarily kicked out of Madame Hohlakhov's apartment for quarreling with him. Even Madame Hohlakhov in her "silliness," perceives Perhotin's character to be vastly superior to Rakitin's. But his shame characteristically impels him in revenge to write another article, published in a periodical significantly entitled "Gossip," in which he scurillously slanders the goodhearted, simple-minded woman. Rakitin is further exposed at the trial during which his grandiloquence about reforming Russia is deflated by the defense attorney's review of his many misdeeds, and by Dmitri's shouting out that Rakitin is a "Bernard," a "contemptible Bernard and opportunist." Further and finally he is disgraced by the testimony of Grushenka, who confesses that Rakitin is in fact her cousin, much to Rakitin's chagrin, but who as a cousin nonetheless regularly borrowed money from her for luxuries, even though he had enough money without her help.

Thus Dostoevsky, one of the most compassionate of novelists, who can communicate compassion for almost all his characters however weak or vile, even characters like Kirillov or Svidrigailov or Rogozhin—or even Old Karamazov himself—cannot muster a single iota of compassion for Rakitin. Rakitin becomes, in fact, a caricature of the Europeanized Russian atheistic liberal, and this poisonous portrayal of the doctrines and deeds of Rakitin is Dostoevsky's way of expressing his contempt for the comfortable atheist intellectual who believes in an earthly paradise without God, a species which in both Russia and Western Europe was then, as later, rife.

But whereas Rakitin goes out into the world to preach that there is no God-and-immortality, Alyosha goes out into the world to preach the good news that there is God-and-immortality. In fact, we are told that if Alyosha had not done so, he would have dedicated his life to socialism (i.e., to the task of setting up a heaven on earth if such were the only heaven man could ever hope to know).

Alyosha is one of the truly remarkable portraits of goodness in all literature. Dostoevsky had had plenty of practice in portraying pure goodness, or nearly pure goodness, during his writing career, and with some success. But Alyosha is not patterned after the sentimentally good characters of *Poor Folk* or *White Nights* or *A Gentle Creature* or *The Insulted and the Injured*, nor is he, any more than Father Zossima, the superhuman character of Prince Myshkin in *The Idiot*. Just as Father Zossima's early life was unsaintly, so, too, Alyosha's life was not without blemish. But whereas Father Zossima's imperfections were due chiefly to unexemplary behavior in his youth, Alyosha's are due principally to imperfections of faith. Being only a budding saint, he lacks Father Zossima's uncanny spiritual insight into people's souls; he nevertheless understands, despite occasional bewilderment, the complexity of Ivan and Dmitri a good deal better than anyone else in the novel, except Father Zossima himself.

But we are to understand that Alyosha possessed unusual qualities of saintliness even as a boy. He was, as Dostoevsky says, "simply an early lover of humanity";

and though "he seemed throughout his life to put implicit trust in people, yet no one ever looked on him as a simpleton or naive person." "There was something about him," we are told, "which made one feel at once (and it was so all his life afterwards) that he did not care to judge of others—that he would never take it upon himself to criticize and would not condemn anyone for anything," not even those who at his father's house performed in the "very sink of filthy debauchery."

Alyosha is thus a perfect spiritual foil to Rakitin. Nor is he the stereotyped ascetic—pale, withdrawn, strange. On the contrary, he is robust and rosy-cheeked. Having learned to overcome the shyness, even sullenness of his youth, he had come to be loved and admired by everyone, at least everyone except Rakitin. Even his father felt a "real and deep affection for him, such as he had never been capable of feeling for anyone before."

In his religious zeal Alyosha puts his soul in the hands of the man whom he conceives to be most nearly like Christ Himself, namely Father Zossima, an elder in the Russian Orthodox tradition of elders. Alyosha regarded him as the most saintly man who ever lived, so that when Zossima dies and his body decomposes prematurely this seemingly reverse miracle for a time shatters his faith.

Actually Dostoevsky uses the phenomenon, not merely of the corruption, but of the *premature* corruption, of Father Zossima's body to test the faith of all who learn of it. The faith of a few, like Father Paissey and Father Iosif, remains steadfast in the face of the event, but many of the monks react shamefully to the phenomenon and indeed some, out of jealousy, even hatred, take it as "a sign from heaven," and cannot conceal their delight that this holy man is not so holy after all, that indeed his doctrine that "life is a great joy and not a vale of tears" is false. Except for the ineffectual Father Iosif, even the monks who were professed followers of Father Zossima do not protest against such interpretations. Father Ferapont, on the other hand, in his fanaticism rushes into the cell, driving out the evil spirits and the visitors, "unclean devils" along with them, and in his self-rightousness launches the unkindest attack of all on Alyosha's saint. Then, having himself been driven out of the cell by Father Paissey, he falls to the ground shouting, "My God has conquered," which performance causes some of the less perceptive brethren to conclude that it is Father Ferapont who is the true saint. When the news of Father Zossima's death spreads, a rush of outside visitors comes into the cell to confirm, with their own eyes, the untimely corporeal decay. Most of these visitors are of "the educated class," who wish to confirm their own unbelief, so that they can say, in effect, "I have seen and therefore I do not believe." Few of the peasantry, on the other hand, are among them; in the strength of their faith they are not seeking evidence against God.

Alyosha, we are to understand, is not like the monks of little faith. He is, on the contrary, "of great faith." His problem is that, in his youthfulness, he worships Father Zossima too much, and Christ not enough; he pays too much attention to the words of Father Zossima and not enough to the words of Scripture. He finds the circumstances of Father Zossima's death particularly hard to take in light of legends that bodies of earlier holy monks in the monastery— Job, who died at age 105, and the "crazy saint," Father Varsonofy —did not decompose, and that further, their dead faces seemed bathed in holy light. In fact, Alyosha was sitting on the grave of Father Job when Father Paissey discovered him. "Can you be

with those of little faith?" he enquired, observing
Alyosha's distress. The answer, alas, is that at this particular moment he is. And he walks out of the monastery
as if protesting against God. When Rakitin accosts him,
to ask him if he really thought that his elder would work
miracles, Alyosha cries out, "I believe, I believe, I want to
believe, and I will believe."

But Alyosha had yet to learn what had to be learned,
namely that faith in God cannot depend upon ocular
evidence, upon miracles in particular, for if there are occasional miracles that may strengthen one's belief, there
are countless "reverse miracles" that weaken it, so that
the net result is bound to be a weakening of faith, not a
strengthening of it. Dostoevsky's point is that one needs
faith to have faith. "Faith does not, in the realist, spring
from the miracle," he observes, "but the miracle from
faith." Alyosha at that moment erred in thinking that
Father Zossima was more like Christ than he actually
was, or that any man can be so much like Christ as
Alyosha supposed Father Zossima to be.

Faith, Dostoevsky maintains, must draw only upon
the miracle of revelation, Scripture, as the mysterious
visitor did when he gave himself up at Father Zossima's
behest, and from love, just as Father Zossima had told
Madame Holakhov: "In as far as you advance in love,
you will grow surer of the reality of God and of the immortality of your soul. If you attain to perfect self-
forgetfulness in the love of your neighbor, then you will
believe without doubt, and no doubt can possibly enter
your soul. This has been tried. This is certain."

There is some irony in the fact that Alyosha's faith,
which is shattered by ocular evidence, is also to be par-
tially restored by ocular evidence. Despite Dostoevsky's
insistence that ocular evidence must not be made the

basis of faith, Alyosha in his despair accepts Grushenka's invitation to ruin him and finds instead that she is to serve him, not so much because she has, in an act of love, taken pity on his sorrow, as that he, in an act of love, takes pity on her sorrow. For she, at that moment, was suffering too: should she forgive her Pole, "her first and rightful lover," and accept his invitation to marry him instead of staying with Dmitri, who was deserting his fiancée for her? "She is more loving than we," he tells Rakitin. "This soul is not yet at peace with itself, one must be tender with it . . . there may be a treasure in that soul." And Grushenka replies: "I knew that someone like you would come and forgive me. I believed that, nasty as I am, someone would really love me, not only with a shameful love." And so she resolves to forgive her "first and rightful lover," and to go to him. There is truth in Rakitin's mocking words as he and Alyosha leave Grushenka's house: "Well, so you've saved the sinner? Have you turned the Magdelene into the true path? Driven out the seven devils, eh? So you see the miracles you are looking out for just now have come to pass." And indeed Grushenka had, as Alyosha said, raised his soul from the depths.

Alyosha knows he has performed no miracle, but he does realize that his own spiritual life has given him the power to strengthen the spiritual life of others, and he returns to the monastery—a symbol of his renewed faith—in time to hear Father Paissey read in Father Zossima's cell the Gospel story of Christ's first miracle at the wedding at Cana. The stench of Father Zossima's decomposing corpse is now so strong that the monastery windows have been opened, but Alyosha is oblivious to it, and as he kneels to pray, he undergoes a kind of spiritual transformation, a revelation, a mystical experience as he hears the description of Christ's first miracle "to help man's gladness." In fact, what he does is take a little transcendental nap and dreams that Father Zossima rises out of his coffin, comes toward him, and speaks to him: "Begin your work, dear one, begin it. Do you see your Son, do you see Him?. . . . He is changing the water into wine that the gladness of the guests may not be cut short. He is expecting new guests." Whereupon Alyosha stretches out his hand, cries out and wakes up; then rising, he goes to Father Zossima's coffin, pauses to look down at the dead man with the icon on his breast and the cross on his peaked cap, and then turns and walks out of the cell. Once outside he takes in the mystery of the earth and the stars, then suddenly throws himself on the ground as if to embrace it, and vows to love it forever. He longs to forgive everyone for everything and to beg forgiveness not only for himself, but for all men. He knows then that "something firm and unshakeable as that vault of heaven" has entered his soul, that indeed "someone visited the monastery to carry on God's work in the world as Father Zossima had bid him."

Dostoevsky's principal aim in this episode is to emphasize that love of man must be based on the love of God; it must be a religious love. As such it contrasts with the humanitarian concept of love proposed by atheistic utopians like Rakitin in the novel and countless others who have concluded that there is no God, and who have begun to preach love of man without God. But as Dostoevsky has been insisting throughout not only this novel but throughout his later years generally, a man is not going to love other men very much if he doesn't first love God. He may love man for man's sake so long as it gives him pleasure and satisfaction, but pleasure and satisfaction run out too soon to keep the outward marks of our humanity—civilization—together, and so faith and love of God are required to supply the deficiency. A perfect faith demands no miracles beyond the miracle of the Scriptures, a faith that is supported not by the actions of men but by the Word of God. Alyosha learns that one may expect miracles from Christ but not from Father Zossima or anyone else, whoever he may be. Christ is God, but man is only man. Alyosha was not transformed by the gospel according to Belinsky or Feuerbach or Chernyshevsky or any of the other successors of the Enlightenment, as Rakitin was, but by the Gospel according to Christ. In short, Dostoevsky is saying that what the world needs is religious faith if the Truth is to be served and, incidentally, civilization is to be preserved.

Thus the way is prepared in the novel to play out the drama of humanitarian love as preached by Rakitin and the "socialists," and of Christian love as preached by Alyosha. The stage for the drama turns out to be the mind and heart of the thirteen-year-old Kolya, who represents the younger generation in Russia and, more broadly, all future generations in civilization everywhere. Rakitin and Alyosha vie, so to speak, for the soul of Kolya, almost as in a medieval morality play.

Just as Alyosha is the budding saint, so Kolya is the budding intellectual, and in his "precocity," he is susceptible to all manner of ideas, wherever they may come from. When Alyosha first meets him, Kolya's ideas happen to come from the Enlighteners like Voltaire and the Russian radicals like Belinsky and Herzen, as interpreted by Rakitin, and he tries them out on Alyosha. With a patronizing tone he assures Alyosha that "contact with real life" will cure him of his belief in God; that it is possible to love mankind without believing in God; that he is

himself in fact a socialist, "an incurable socialist"; that
Christianity has been of use only to the rich and powerful
and that it has kept the lower classes in slavery; that if
Christ were alive today He would be "found in the ranks
of the revolutionists." At the same time, he insists that he
often disagrees with Rakitin, that in fact he has nothing
against God, ("I admit that He is needed . . . for the order
of the universe and all that") and that in fact if there were
no God He would have to be invented. Furthermore, in
his liberality he points out that he is not opposed to
Christ, for he was "a most humane person." He confesses
too that he wants to remain in Russia rather than go to
America as "they" have been urging him to do, and that
he wants to be of great service to humanity. Finally, he
asks to hear Alyosha's arguments against these views,
for, he says, "I want to hear both sides."

Alyosha recognizes that Kolya is not expressing his
own ideas, "What fools have you made friends with?" he
exclaims, and he expresses sadness to Kolya that "a
charming nature such as yours should be perverted by all
this crude nonsense before you have begun life."

But ultimately Alyosha wins Kolya over not so much
with his mind as with his heart, for Alyosha understands
him in something of the same way that Father Zossima
understood those who came to him for spiritual help.
When Kolya expresses his deep regret that he did not
make up with Alyosha sooner and that it was out of con-
ceit and "beastly wilfulness" that he did not do so, Alyosha
reassures him that he does indeed have a charming, if
distorted nature. When Kolya learns that Alyosha, whom
he secretly admires, not only does not despise him but on
the contrary loves and admires him, Kolya's heart melts
and he too expresses his love and admiration for Alyosha.
The following exchange indicates how enthusiastically

and how thoroughly he is won over to Alyosha's side, which is to say the side of God-and-immortality:

> "You know, Kolya, you will be very unhappy in your life," something made Alyosha say suddenly.
>
> "I know, I know. How you know it all beforehand!" Kolya agreed at once.
>
> "But you will bless life on the whole, all the same."
>
> "Just so, Hurrah! Do you know, what delights me most is that you treat me like an equal. But we are not equals, no we are not, you are better! But we shall get on."

And so Alyosha, the believer, snatches the soul of Kolya from Rakitin, the unbeliever, and thus performs his first good work in the world after his spiritual purification. The scene becomes a miniature of how the believers are going to save Russia, indeed the world, from the unbelievers.

Thus the way is prepared for the grand finale of the novel, for there Kolya, in his youthful manner, expresses the desire to do good for all humanity, regardless of what others think. The last scene fittingly returns to a discussion of the question of God-and-immortality, which is the overriding subject of the novel, this time between Alyosha and the boys. "Can it be true," Kolya asks Alyosha, "what's taught us in religion, that we shall rise again from the dead and shall live and see each other again?" "Certainly we shall all rise again," Alyosha replies, "certainly we shall see each other and tell each other with joy and gladness all that has happened." "Ah, how splendid it will be!" exlaims Kolya.

And then come the ringing words and by now the celebrated words, first from Kolya and then from all the boys: "Hurrah for Karamazov!" expressing with greater rhetorical force in *The Brothers Karamzov* or perhaps in any other novel the eventual victory of the saving power of belief in God-and-immortality over the destructive powers of unbelief which Dostoevsky with all the energies and power and genius at his command had tried to demonstrate. For Kolya's cry at the end affirms above all that there is God-and-immortality, and since there is, there is also virtue and not everything is lawful. It affirms that goodness has an absolute meaning beyond the pleasure of the one who performs it and the one who receives it, that there is a meaning and a value to Dmitri's not taking advantage of Katerina, and a meaning to his desire to return the 3,000 rubles, even though Katerina, would readily forgive him if he didn't; that there is a meaning to Katerina's own shame in offering herself to Dmitri in return for 4,500 rubles to save her father; a meaning to the mysterious visitor's confessing his crime even though there was no earthly need to; a meaning to Dmitri's suffering in Siberia, indeed to everyone's suffering, even the suffering of the innocent babes that Ivan so vividly described; a meaning to Captain Snegiryov's refusing the 200 rubles even though his family's and his own life and fortunes depended upon it; a meaning to Grushenka's guilt, which stemmed from her seducer; a meaning to Zossima's refusal to kill though his refusal seemed to disgrace his regiment; a meaning to Markel's conversation on his death-bed; a meaning to Ivan's confession at the trial of his part in the murder of his father; and indeed a meaning to all the deeds done in the novel, both good and bad. Kolya's cry is above all an affirmation that man is a spritual creature, and therefore not a beast, that the main purpose of life is not comfort and pleasure but goodness and, inevitably, suffering. It is an affirmation that man draws his dignity not from himself or from other men, including the state, but rather from

God, and that his dignity therefore cannot be destroyed. It is, in short, a symbol of the triumph of belief over unbelief, the triumph of God over Satan, the triumph of man over himself, in spite of himself.

CHAPTER VII

COMRADE DOSTOEVSKY

The atheism that Dostoevsky fought against in his mature novels had its origin in Western Europe, but it has thus far enjoyed its greatest political triumph in Eastern Europe, especially in Dostoevsky's own country. Leading 19th-century Russian atheists like Belinsky, Dobrolyubov, Chernyshevsky, and Pisarev were children of the leading atheists of France and England and especially Germany. Not all of the utopians of 19th-century Europe were atheists, but the more atheistic they were the more the Russian intellectuals were drawn to them because they themselves tended toward the most extreme radicalism as a reaction to the extreme conservatism of their church and their government. By the time the works of Marx reached the ears and eyes of Russian intellectuals his way had been well prepared. The objections of Marx and Engels to religion were not notably different from the objections of atheistic utopians who had preceded them. Religion was first of all anti-rational and supra-scientific and hence would not submit to the demands of naked reason or naked science. Second, religion appeared to impede progress in this life by its emphasis upon the next life, for the goal of religion was not comfort but goodness. Third, religion appeared to best serve the interests of oppressors and to foster class exploitation. Fourth, and most important, it threatened the authority of the state by professing to possess an authority that went beyond the state.

Lenin's hostility toward religion actually surpassed that of Marx himself, for whereas Marx regarded religion merely as "the opium of the people," Lenin's language on the subject of religion in his letters to Gorky and elsewhere strained the reaches of his rhetoric to the breaking point. His statement that "every idea of God" is "unutterable vileness" may serve as a sample.

This is not the place to describe how Lenin made atheism a policy of state or how a few months after the Revolution he issued a decree which was ultimately aimed at the destruction of all religion in the Soviet Union. Nor is it necessary here to describe the more-or-less relentless crusade against religion that was conducted in the years following and is still being conducted today. It is enough perhaps to say that nowhere before in the whole history of the world has atheism been so well organized, so belligerent, and so bent on destroying systematically all religious influence than in the Soviet Union.

It is therefore of particular interest to an understanding of both Dostoevsky and of the Soviet Union to examine how Dostoevsky's reputation has fared in his native land since the Bolshevik Revolution.

The official Soviet view in recent times is reflected fairly faithfully in the way Dostoevsky is presented to students in Soviet schools. In the first place, none of his works appear in the literary textbooks in any grade in Soviet schools, as opposed to a rich representation of Pushkin, Gogol, Turgenev, Tolstoy, and Chekhov, as well as a fairly large number of lesser writers at all grade levels, often with detailed biographical sketches.

It is true, of course, that Dostoevsky was not exactly a children's writer. Even his story entitled "A Christmas Tree and a Wedding" is chiefly about a dirty old man, and "The Little Hero" deals with sexual precocity. His pious piece entitled "A Boy at Christ's Christmas Tree" might seem a good thing for children, but since it suggests that the only sure relief from poverty is in Heaven, it does not exactly square with the Soviet view of things. No one could object to Dostoevsky's little sketch entitled "The Peasant Marey," but so light a story hardly suggests that Dostoevsky is one of the greatest writers of all time, and, relatively speaking, it is hardly worthwhile mentioning even to Soviet students.

There are, of course, numerous passages in Dostoevsky's novels that make eminently good reading for younger students, especially perhaps certain episodes in Book X of *The Brothers Karamazov*, which is entitled "The Children." Actually in 1947 Detgiz (State Publishers of Children's Literature) published these episodes in *Schoolboy's Library*, but the book was sharply criticized because of Alyosha's religious orientation and because it misrepresented the younger generation. In 1971, however, appeared a fairly large printing of *Dostoevsky for Children* with a selection of his works together with a biography of Dostoevsky, the first that had ever been written specifically for children.

But the literature textbooks used in Soviet schools do not customarily include short excerpts from long works, and there is some doubt that the compilers wished to encourage students to look further into such novels as *The Possessed* and *The Brothers Karamazov*. The conclusion seems to have been that if Soviet schools cannot parade Dostoevsky with pride, as they can Pushkin and Tolstoy, he ought not to be paraded at all.

Soviet students, however, who get as far as the 9th grade (about 30 percent) do encounter Dostoevsky in their textbook *Russkaya Literatura*, which is a literary history of Russia from 1860 to 1900. This text contains separate chapters on Goncharov (53 pages), Ostrovsky (20 pages), Turgenev (25 pages), Chernyshevsky (30 pages), Nekrassov (44 pages), Saltykov-Shchedrin (22 pages), Tolstoy (55 pages), and Chekhov (35 pages). Buried in a chapter entitled "The Seventies and Eighties" are 6 pages devoted to Dostoevsky, along with a page or two each about Leskov and Garshin, and a few remarks about Russian art, sculpture, and music.

To be sure, there is the famous but cropped portrait of Dostoevsky by the artist Perov, and there is a brief sketch of the details of Dostoevsky's life with special emphases on the episode which sent him to prison for revolutionary activities against the Czar. He is referred to as a "famous Russian writer" and most of his substantial works are at least mentioned, though not *Notes from the Underground. Poor Folk* and *The Insulted and the Injured* get special attention as exposés of the plight of the poor in Czarist times. *Memoirs from a Deadhouse* gets some notice because it "inevitably directs the reader's thoughts to an evaluation of the cruel social structure which destroyed the spiritual wealth of the Russian people."

In an analysis of *Crime and Punishment*, which takes up two of the six pages, students are told that Raskolnikov "sees the sharp contrasts in the way of life of people in a capitalist city, but he seeks the solution not in organized struggle against the social-political structure, but in a personal revolt against existing laws and popular morality." Sonya's solution, the text says, is "Christian humility and purification of the soul through suffering."

It points out that there is an "obvious falseness to the
basic idea" of the novel because "it looks for a way out of
social injustice not in revolutionary struggle against the
social structure, but in religious humility." The analysis
ends by telling Soviet students, however, that "the
powerful realistic treatment of social controversies in the
age of capitalism and the deep and precise psychological
analysis in the work made *Crime and Punishment* one of
the remarkable phenomena of Russian and world literature."

The Idiot and The Raw Youth are mentioned only by
title, but *The Possessed* gets a paragraph in which Soviet
students are told that characters like Pyotr Verhovensky,
Stavrogin, and Karamazinov, are clearly caricatures of
revolutionary, social, and literary leaders of the time,
specifically of Petrashevsky, Nechaiev, Speshnev, and
Turgenev. *The Possessed* "is a hostile attack against
specific persons and the progressive course of Russian
culture. The socialist view of the progressive activity of
the times, the materialistic philosophy, and the revolutionary ideas which transformed society are all
misrepresented in the novel and the legacy of Belinsky,
Chernyshevsky, and Dobrolyubov is rejected outright."

The Brothers Karamazov gets four short paragraphs.
It is referred to as "one of the most famous" of Dostoevsky's works, the basic theme of which is "the degenera-
tion and moral collapse of a noble family." Old Karamazov and his sons, Ivan and Dmitri, demonstrate "how
the corrupting power of money drives a whole family . . .
to total moral destruction." Dostoevsky, the text goes on
to say, "is faced in the novel with the problem of convincing the reader that salvation from the terrors of life can
be found only in religion," and it objects to his view of
"the lofty and all-powerful role of religion" in the novel.

A revealing summary of Dostoevsky's works in general then follows:

> There is more than a little that is controversial and false in the works of Dostoevsky, but the progressive reader clearly outstrips the writer in his view of the problems and characer of the social struggle. Dostoevsky's error consisted in the fact that he attempted to solve the tormenting social questions on a psychological level rather than on a social level.
>
> But despite all his false, utopian theories, the realism in the works of Dostoevsky always took precedence over his reactionary views. The power of his talent as a portrayer of morals and manners, his mastery of profound psychological analysis, his deep sympathy for the plight of "the insulted and the injured," and for the little people, have called universal attention to Dostoevsky and have earned him world-wide renown.

The text points out that Gorky compared Dostoevsky to Shakespeare and that Lenin, although he attacked Dostoevsky mercilessly for the "false tendencies" of his works, especially in *The Possessed*, admitted that Dostoevsky was a genius and that he considered *Memoirs from a Deadhouse* to be "unsurpassed in Russian and world literature not only as a picture of prison life but as a reflection of the 'dead house' in which the Russian people lived under the Romanov dynasty."

The textbook ends the discussion of Dostoevsky with two paragraphs from an article in *Pravda* entitled "A Great Russian Writer," written in honor of the 75th anniversary of Dostoevsky's death. "The characters that the writer created," says the article, "demonstrated at times such a penetrating spirit of protest against social injustice, hatred for the indignities of man, and belief in his high calling that they not only weakened but even stifled the reactionary ideas in his works." And it concludes with the observation that even until the last days of his life Dostoevsky suffered from a "cruel inner struggle" resulting from the contradictory elements in his world view.

Altogether the treatment accorded Dostoevsky in Soviet schools may well leave students wondering why Dostoevsky in this textbook, which was first published in is one of the world's great writers. On the other hand, they may even be led to believe that any of 20 or 30 Russian writers are better writers than Dostoevsky.

The fact is, however, that the treatment accorded Dostoevsky in this textbook, which was first published in 1956, reflects his rehabilitation, which was just getting underway. During the 1920's, Dostoevsky scholars took advantage of the relatively free intellectual atmosphere in the Soviet Union, and his works and studies of his works appeared in fairly large quantities. A tightening up in the 1930's, however, severely curtailed scholarly and critical activity on Dostoevsky. Then, after a brief patriotic revival of interest in Dostoevsky during World War II, which emphasized his Russianness rather than his religiousness, the spirit of Zhdanovism took over, and between the years 1947 and 1955, not a single book on Dostoevsky was published in the Soviet Union. With the easing of literary controls in the Soviet Union in 1956, critics and scholars sought to resurrect Dostoevsky's name, but the difficulty was that the resurrection could not proceed in the face of Lenin's disapproval.

Despite the nice things Lenin had said about Dostoevsky as quoted in the 9th-grade textbook, his true feelings about Dostoevsky were believed (until 1955) to be the ones recorded in *Meetings with Lenin* by N. Valentinov, whom Lenin knew well, and who told him that the works of Dostoevsky are "trash' and that having read *Memoirs from a Deadhouse* and *Crime and Punishment* he had no desire to read *The Possessed* or *The Brothers Karamazov*. "I know the contents of both these putrid works," he told Valentinov, "and that's quite enough for me. I was going to read *The Brothers Karamazov*, but I gave it up—the scenes in the monastery made me sick. As for *The Devils*, it's a nasty, thoroughly reactionary piece of work."

A scanning of the collected works of Lenin yielded no favorable reference to Dostoevsky whatsoever. Then suddenly the year was saved by the publication in 1955 of an article by Vladimir Bonch-Breuvich, one of Lenin's collaborators, entitled "Lenin on Books and Authors," in which the author claimed that Lenin was not as hostile to Dostoevsky as had been supposed, but actually "had a high regard for Dostoevsky's talent." In fact, the references to Lenin's attitude toward Dostoevsky as they are represented in the 9th-grade textbook cited above were taken from Bonch-Breuvich's article. The 75th-anniversary celebration could now proceed with governmental blessing, and a flood of Dostoevsky's works began to appear, including separate editions of *The Insulted and the Injured*, *Crime and Punishment*, *The Idiot*, and *The Raw Youth*.

A spate of articles also appeared in honor of the event and almost all of them were entitled "A Great Russian Writer," because they were almost all modeled on an article in *Pravda* (for February 6, 1956) entitled "A Great Russian Writer." Since the article was unsigned it took on the character of an editorial and hence more or less represented the new official view of Dostoevsky. In fact, it is this article that is quoted in the 9th-grade textbook, and since it discusses many of Dostoevsky's major works, the analyses of *Crime and Punishment*, *The Possessed* and *The Brothers Karamazov*, which appear in the 9th-grade textbook draw heavily from this article. One can thus feel secure in knowing that Soviet students are getting the Party view of Dostoevsky.

In general, this new estimate of Dostoevsky carried with it the cautionary message that Dostoevsky is indeed a good writer but that he is also a bad thinker. But as the excerpt from the textbook on page 147 suggests, the official view came to be that his good writing more than offset his bad thinking, and that although his orientation was reactionary (i.e., religious), his deep devotion to the downtrodden, his awareness of the evils of wealth, his indignation against injustice, as well as his vast sympathy for mankind generally made the gamble to restore him to respectability seem worthwhile. Plans therefore proceeded for a 10-volume edition of his works, which came out between 1956 and 1958, and for the publication of the fourth volume of his correspondence, which included his most dangerous years, 1878–1881, the first three volumes having been published respectively in 1928, 1930, and 1934.

In the last few years the Soviet Union's publishing record on Dostoevsky has achieved new heights of sophistication, for not only does it include two sumptuous volumes of hitherto unpublished material by Dostoevsky in the *Literaturnoye Nasledstvo* (Literary Heritage) series, and numerous separate editions of his works, but in fact, as a recent article in *Pravda* pointed out, there have been 229 Soviet publications of Dostoevsky's works in 25 languages and 20 million copies in the Soviet Union over the past 20 years. As the crowning glory the Academy (i.e., definitive) Edition of Dostoevsky's complete collected works in 30 volumes is in process of publication, though only about 37,000 copies are to be issued and all by subsription, so that the edition does not come close to meeting Soviet demand.

All this is not to say that the Soviet Union has at last taken Dostoevsky to its bosom, for it has not. It has merely concluded that the advantages of letting him into the light outweigh the advantages of storing him in the dark.

With all the revitalization of interest in Dostoevsky there has, of course, been a multiplication of Dostoevsky scholars in the Soviet Union; but they are often at a loss to know whether to blame him more for his bad thinking or to praise him for his great artistry. Maxim Gorky, who had become the virtual arbiter of literature in the Soviet Union, did not offer much help. For although Gorky had insisted that Dostoevsky's genius is "indisputable," and that he could indeed be compared only to Shakespeare, he also relentlessly attacked Dostoevsky as a thinker both before and after the Revolution. In any case, Soviet scholars and critics are now forced by the facts to recognize that Dostoevsky was a great artist and by the government to recognize that he was a bad thinker.

In good part as a result of Gorky's split judgment, there is a temptation to divide Soviet critics into two sorts: those who play down Dostoevsky's thinking in order to elevate his art, and those who ignore his art in order to expose his thinking. Before examining this phenomenon, however, I should like to emphasize that it was also Russian critics who first recognized that Dostoevsky was both a great artist *and* a great thinker. Such Russian scholars, for example, as Shestov, Rosanov, Merezhkovsky, Ivanov, Zander, Mochulsky, Zenkovsky, Fr. S. Bulgakov, Lossky, Rostislav, and

Pletnev have insisted upon examining Dostoevsky's works within the religious framework of his thought, on the grounds that he cannot be understood otherwise. Scholars such as these have done much to communicate the view that Dostoevsky's religious orientation is in fact his great strength rather than his great weakness, though many of these critics, it is true, either wrote before the Revolution or from the vantage point of emigrés; and some of them, in expressing their enthusiasm for Dostoevsky's thought, did not say enough about his art.

Western scholars, particularly American and English scholars, have, on the other hand, until quite recently, tended to underplay Dostoevsky's religious orientation, either under the influence of 20th-century formalist techniques in criticism or under the impression that Dostoevsky's thinking was so bad that the less said about it the better. It is only recently that a few English and American critics have sympathetically turned attention to Dostoevsky as religious thinker.

But of the Soviet critics who have done most to warn against the dangers of Dostoevsky's thought rather than ponder the pleasures of his art is very likely V. V. Er- milov, whose view of Dostoevsky was whatever the of- ficial view of the moment happened to be; but since the official view of Dostoevsky as a thinker was mostly negative, Ermilov was able to make something of a pro- fession of attacking Dostoevsky's thinking and often in the role of a more or less official spokesman. When Soviet scholars got the nod to resume work on Dostoev- sky, Ermilov was in the vanguard with a book in 1956 entitled *F. M. Dostoevsky*, which he was directed to write by Soviet authorities as an official view of Dostoev- sky as a thinker. The whole book was calculated to alert Soviet readers to the extent to which Dostoevsky's thinking is incompatible with Communist thinking, and it is therefore a rather long book. Ermilov takes the reader on an epistemological tour of Dostoevsky's works, stopping for especially close looks at his mature novels. He warns the reader against Dostoevsky's glorification of Christian humility, of salvation through suffering, of the "religious lie," and against Dostoevsky's whole Christian interpretation of the meaning of life. Despite the fact that he sometimes betrays a massive ignorance of Christian doctrine, Ermilov is acutely aware of Dostoevsky's own devotion to Christian doctrine and the Christian framework of his mature novels.

But Ermilov insists that a writer's art cannot be separated from his thinking, and he therefore concludes that Dostoevsky's bad thinking contaminated his art, so that he finds a steady artistic deteriortion in Dostoevsky from *Poor Folk* to *The Brothers Karamazov*, in the latter of which he claims that Dostoevsky's art had virtually withered away. "His ties with reaction," said Ermilov, "had a ruinous effect both on his artistic veracity as a writer and on the humanistic aspirations in his works." "We Soviet people," he warns, "cannot, however highly we may value his artistic talent, 'forget' or 'forgive' Dosteovsky for the glowering spite which was expressed in his most tendentiously reactionary works, and which blinded him against the best democratic forces of his age. Nor can we forget that even in our times the forces of reaction—Churchmen and other obscurantists—try to exploit his works to promote their own nefarious goals."

Ermilov was not, of course, the only critic in Russia to be more interested in Dostoevsky's bad thinking than in his great art. The tradition dates all the way back to Belinsky, who, after a misreading of *Poor Folk*, pronounced it with great enthusiasm as "the first attempt at

a social novel," but who after a proper reading of
Dostoevsky's next three works, concluded that Dostoevsky was not writing "social novels" after all, and ended
up objecting seriously to them in good part on ideological
grounds. Mikhailovsky, too, in an essay published a year
after Dostoevsky's death labeled him the "cruel talent"
and proceeded to attack his "reactionary views," his
slander of revolutionaries, particularly in *The Possessed*,
and to reject his whole Christian orientation. In fact,
Mikhailovsky's influence on Gorky was so strong that
Gorky on balance must be said to be far more against
Dostoevsky than for him. There followed in the wake of
these authorities a whole series of Marxist and Soviet
critics who were more interested in attacking Dostoevsky's thought than in praising his art. When the spirit of
Zhdanovism overcame Russian literature in 1946, D. I.
Zaslavsky produced an article entitled "Against Idealiza-
tion of the Reactionary Views of Dostoevsky," which appeared in *Kul'tura i Zhizn* (Culture and Life), an official
organ of the Communist Party. In this article Zaslavsky
refused to believe that Dostoevsky was ever a disciple of
Belinsky, and he pointed out that even to the end he opposed revolution and socialism and championed the
monarchy and the Church. In the process he lambasted
those Soviet critics who either ignore Dostoevsky's
ideology or who attempt to turn it to Soviet advantage.

Zaslavsky's more-or-less official warning against the
blandishments of Dostoevsky's thought was immediately
reinforced by an article by Ermilov himself, published in
Lituraturnaya Gazeta, of which he was the editor. In this
article Ermilov not only took back any kind words he
might previously have said about Dostoevsky but
launched a new and even more ferocious attack upon

Dostoevsky's ideology with special emphasis upon exposing Dostoesky's view that natural man is not good enough to get along without God. Dostoevsky, he says, "squandered the whole of his talent in proving the weakness, sinfulness and criminality of human nature." In the process he attacked Dostoevsky's whole Christian orientation and warned other Soviet critics, such as Dolinin and Kirpotin, that there was no way they could justify Dostoevsky's ideology as a support for Soviet Communism. The influence of these two articles by Zaslavsky and Ermilov were enough virtually to silence Dostoevsky scholarship for a period of about nine years until his qualified rehabilitation in 1956.

And yet for all the warnings of party writers against Dostoevsky, it must be said that the weight of Soviet criticisms about Dostoevsky's works since his restoration in 1956 has been thrown in the direction of de-emphasizing his thought and praising his art. There is something rather ironic in this phenomenon because theoretically Soviet criticism must concern itself first of all with the ideological content of literary works. Nonetheless, since 1956 there has been a flood of studies on Dostoevsky's diction, images, style, structure, methodology, and other aspects of his writings which enable critics to more or less concentrate on how Dostoevsky wrote rather than what he thought.

The phenomenon is explainable in part by the fact that more and more the model for Soviet criticism of Dostoevsky has become the works of M. M. Bakhtin, particularly his book entitled *Problems of Dostoevsky's Writing*, which was first published in 1929 and which was republished in a revised and much enlarged edition in 1963 and again in 1972. (An English-language edition was published by Ardis Publishers in 1973.) In analyzing Dostoevsky's works, Bakhtin proposed his theory that Dostoevsky was writing polyphonic novels in which his heroes are allowed to present their dialectic but that Dostoevsky himself presents no dialectic, and that he therefore presents no serious ideological problem. Bakhtin has thus placed himself in the position of quoting and having to agree with the indefensible conclusion of Viktor Shklovsky in his book *Pro and Contra: Remarks on Dostoevsky*, in which he says, "Dostoevsky died without having resolved anything, avoiding solutions, and remaining unreconciled." Bakhtin, it is true, declared that his own criticism was not formalist, or at least not narrowly formalist, but in effect it is formalist, for one cannot get from his criticism very much of what Dostoevsky really thought because Bakhtin does not really think that Dostoevsky was trying to communicate what he thought. If one wishes to compare Bakhtin's book with, for example, Vyasheslav Ivanov's *Dostoevsky and the Tragedy-Novel*, which Bakhtin did not much like, and in which Ivanov recognizes that Dostoevsky takes a strong ideological position, and shows how Dostoevsky's art is dependent upon his thought and vice versa, one may perceive that Bakhtin is far gone in formalism.

As false and indefensible as Bakhtin's method of interpreting Dostoevsky is, it is, however, in the Soviet Union, also safe, and it enables Soviet scholarship on Dostoesky to thrive and even to make substantial contributions to our understanding of his art. The very titles of some of the most important studies on Dostoevsky since 1956 indicate the new emphasis upon form and the new de-emphasis upon his thought, as for example, *On Dostoevsky's Style* by Nikolai Chirkov (1967), *Dostoev-*

sky's Realism by G. M. Fridlender (1964), and *Aesthetics in the Writings of Dostoevsky* by A. P. Belik.

Such efforts to neutralize Dostoevsky as a thinker in the spirit of Bakhtin were somewhat abetted by O. Zundelovich's book *The Novels of Dostoevsky*, in which the author tried to show that, although in the abstract Dostoevsky was a reactionary and a religious dogmatist, in his art he actually rejected his ideology by the very force of his faithful representation of how life really is. In other words he tried to show that Dostoevsky is not really saying what he is saying. Dolinin, on the other hand, one of the most venerable of all Dostoevsky scholars in the Soviet Union, in his book *Dostoevsky's Last Novels*, believes that Dostoevsky's thought and art do indeed coincide; but he undertakes to demonstrate that Dostoevsky, though no flaming liberal, is, on the other hand, not nearly so religious or so reactionary in *The Raw Youth* and *The Brothers Karamazov* as previous Soviet scholarship had said that he is and that he in fact is. Still another attempt to clean up Dostoevsky's thought is a book by Iuri Kudriavtsev *Rebellion or Religion* (1970) in which he bravely, if pathetically, challenges Nikolai Berdyaev's interpretation of Dostoevsky.

Thus one may say that Soviet criticism, since the liberation of Dostoevsky from Zhdanov's prison, has employed a variety of ruses to avoid facing the facts about what Dostoevsky was really trying to tell his countrymen. In the face of such handicaps there is still a good deal that is valuable in recent Dostoevsky criticism in the Soviet Union, but the truth about Dostoevsky has not yet come out in them. Ermilov and Zaslavsky are not sophisticated critics compared to many of those cited here, but they understand what Dostoevsky is saying and they understand it well enough to know that what he is saying in his mature novels is not in the best interests of the Soviet Union.

Three of Dostoevsky's novels in particular tear at the puffy underside of Communist theory and expose the dark skeleton within, namely *Notes from the Underground*, *The Possessed*, and *The Brothers Karamazov*, and it is with good reason that the Soviet government has been reluctant to publish them. The later correspondence of Dostoevsky and *The Diary of a Writer*, both written during Dostoevsky's most thoughtful years, also appeared under protest, but it is the three novels—precisely because they are novels and novels by one of the world's most powerful writers—that are considered most dangerous, particularly in a country that values the written word perhaps more than any other country in the world. In 1956 when the two-volume collection of his short novels and stories appeared in a printing of 150,000 copies, *Notes from the Underground* was omitted. And even among the editors of the 1956 10-volume edition of Dostoevsky's works, there occurred a heated debate as to whether *Notes from the Underground* should be included. The outcome was that it should be, on the grounds that its omission would be too obvious, though it was felt that the crucial episode of Stavrogin's confession, in the chapter entitled "At Tikhon's" in *The Possessed*, might safely be left out. The attacks on these three novels and the warnings against them have been stronger than on *Crime and Punishment*, *The Idiot*, *The Raw Youth* or any of Dostoevsky's other novels and stories written either early or late in his life.

Notes from the Underground, despite its brevity, is in some ways the most ferocious attack of all upon what came to be the fundamental principles and premises of

Soviet Communism. The Underground Man insists that man's perverseness and irrational drives and desires "cause every system and every theory to crumble on contact," and he strikes at the very heart of Communist theory. Dostoevsky in this work is merely reminding us all that human nature is what 5,000 years of history confirm it to be, that it has not notably progressed and will not notably progress to the point that it can thrive in an atheist Communist society. And if the crucial omitted passage in which Dostoevsky "deduced from all this the necessity of faith and Christ" had been preserved, then *Notes from the Underground* would no doubt be doubly anathema to Soviet interests. But even without this passage the truths about human nature which Dostoevsky insisted upon in *Notes from the Underground* will not go away precisely because they are truths, and they are truths with which no Communist society can cope very long without moving farther and farther away from the utopia it hopes to achieve.

The Possessed, of all Dostoevsky's works, has the honor of being the most reviled in the Soviet Union, chiefly because it attempts to show what the consequences of revolution can be in the hands of atheist intellectuals. No separate edition of it has appeared since 1958. In a sense those who complain that *The Possessed* caricatures the 19th-century socialist utopian radicals are right, for, as usual, it was Dostoevsky's technique to work with extremes of human behavior and human ideas in order to define the essence of them. *The Possessed* is a telling demonstration that without religion, revolutionaries can logically and indeed with moral impunity undertake any measures whatsoever at whatever cost in human life and human suffering, provided they appear to fulfill the dreams of naive idealists like Shigalov, or cynical opportunists like Pyotr (who is possessed with a drive for raw power). And yet the political extermination of millions of Soviet citizens in the 1930's makes Pyotr Verhovensky a candidate for sainthood compared to Stalin.

But as we have seen, it was in *The Brothers Karamazov* that Dostoevsky most devastatingly demonstrated the untenability of this idea with every ounce of his gigantic intellectual and artistic powers.

Perhaps this discussion of Comrade Dostoevsky may properly end with a summary of the basic differences between the premises of Communism and the premises of Dostoevsky: Communism holds that man's worth is imputed to him not by God but by the State; Dostoevsky holds that man's worth is imputed to him not by the State but by God. Communism holds that man is naturally good and that religion weakens him; Dostoevsky holds that man is naturally weak and that religion strengthens him. Communism believes that reason-and-science must be the ultimate source of truth; Dostoevsky believes that the Bible must be the ultimate source of truth. Communism believes that a heaven-on-earth can be achieved without God; Dostoevsky believes that a heaven-on-earth can be achieved only with God.

These differences are so fundamental, so irreconcilable, and so far-reaching in their implications that the only way Dostoevsky can accommodate Communism or Communism accommodate Dostoevsky is to play them both down or to pretend that they don't exist. But to play them down or to pretend that they don't exist is to ignore the very essence of both Dostoevsky and Communism.

CHAPTER VIII

DOSTOEVSKY AND
THE CONTEMPORARY WORLD

Although Communism is a powerful atheistic force in the world today, the Communist world is not the whole world, and the fact is that atheism, however unorganized, is now thriving quite as well outside the Communist world as it is in it, and its roots in the Western world go far deeper. This fertile forest of unbelief did not result from the labors of the masses; its trees were planted in hothouses by the intellectuals of the 17th century and were assiduously watered and cultivated by the intellectuals of succeeding centuries until by endless transplantations their shade now spreads over virtually everyone in the Western world. In discussing the relevance of Dostoevsky's thought to the problem of contemporary unbelief, there may be some value in identifying two species of unbelief which appear to dominate the thinking of intellectuals today, namely atheistic existentialism and atheistic humanism.

Dostoevsky and the Existentialists

Despite whatever certain contemporary thinkers have in common that justifies calling them existentialists, the fact remains that believing existentialists, such as Kirkegaard and Gabriel Marcel and Rudolph Bultmann, are so far removed in their thinking from unbelieving existentialists, such as Heidegger and Sartre and Merleau-Ponty, that their similarities are relatively inconsequential. The overriding difference is that the believing existentialists recognize the Personhood and supremacy of God, whereas the unbelieving existentialists recognize only the personhood and supremacy of man. As we have seen, Dostoevsky, who has himself been linked with the existentialists, insisted that it makes literally all the difference in the world whether the ultimate moral authority comes from God or merely from man, and he profoundly distrusted the ultimate authority of man for reasons which he spent the better part of his genius trying to communicate. We have seen, too, that Dostoevsky insisted that morality depends upon religion, which, in turn, to be very effective for very long, must be based upon belief not merely in God but in God-and-immortality, which in turn cannot be perpetuated in any effective way except through the authority of Sacred Scripture—and ultimately of the Church.

It is true that, like Dostoevsky, the atheist existentialists have punctured the puny life raft of reason-and-science which had kept the atheist (and deist) intellectuals of the 18th and 19th centuries afloat. But more important, unlike Dostoevsky, they reject the authority of revelation and hence any super-human basis for morality. Furthermore, the atheist existentialists have so far beat out their believing brethren that the phrase "atheistic existentialism" has become a tautology, just as "atheistic communism" is a tautology. It turns out that, after Kirkegaard, the works of believing existentialists such as Maritain, Marcel, Martin Buber, and Karl Barth were minor setbacks in the onward march of unbelieving existentialists from Heidegger to Sartre and beyond.

As the thickening mantle of unbelief began to settle on the world, existentialism and Marxism—the latter the most powerful species of atheistic humanism—have emerged as the dominating philosophies of the 20th century. The two are rival philosophies, and despite the intellectual gymnastics of such writers as Sartre and Merleau-Ponty to reconcile them, they remain essentially irreconcilable. Yet, viewed in the broadest perspective, they are in fact both on the same side of the philosophical coin. What Marxism and atheistic existentialism have most in common is their atheism. Both deny the existence of God-and-immortality and hence insist that the only world is this world. Both deny the validity and authority of biblical revelation and both therefore insist that the highest truth is man-made truth, and that man's dignity is imputed to him by man, not God, and therefore may be destroyed by man. The differences between Marxism and atheistic existentialism, which historians and philosophers like to emphasize, if viewed in a wide enough perspective, become relatively inconsequential. The other side of the philosophical coin is the world of religion, a largely invisible world, a world of the spirit, literally, not figuratively, including the Christian world, the world of Dostoevsky, a world which looks to another world, a world which believes that the highest truth is God's truth, a world which insists that man's dignity, his worth, is imputed to him by God, and is therefore guaranteed.

Something of the similarities and differences between the Communist and the atheistic existentialist world on the one hand and the Christian world on the other can perhaps be illustrated by a story entitled *How the Soviet Robinson Was Created*, which was written by the Soviet authors Ilf and Petrov. The story is a magnificent spoof on the doctrine of Socialist Realism, which informs all proper Soviet literature, but it has far-reaching philosophical implications which are helpful to the discussion here.

The story tells about a writer named Moldovantsev who had been commissioned by the editor of a literary magazine to write a novel about a Soviet Robinson Crusoe. After the editor had read it over, he complained to Moldovantsev that there was nothing "Soviet" about the story; it was merely the Robinson Crusoe story all over again, except that Robinson was a Soviet citizen. The editor thereupon made a number of suggestions for revision. He proposed that in addition to the other items tossed up on shore by the waves, there should also be the members of a Mestcom (the local Trade Union Committee) including a chairman and a lady dues-collector. He proposed further that the lady dues-collector could marry Robinson or perhaps the chairman, provided that their love was chaste. The editor also suggested that the waves should cast up a fireproof safe in which the dues could be kept as well as a conference table with a green cover to be used for meetings of the Mestcom. Moldovantsev reluctantly agreed to these changes; but when the editor insisted that the waves should also toss up the masses, "the broad strata of the toilers," Moldovantsev objected that a single wave can't cast up thousands of people. Whereupon the editor suggested that the island be changed to a peninsula, and that the whole idea of a shipwreck be abandoned. As a final change he proposed that Moldovantsev eliminate Robinson from the story on the grounds that he is an "incongruous, utterly unjustified figure of a chronic bellyacher." The story ends as

Moldovantsev promises to go home and write the novel all over again, and this time do it right.

The hypothetical problem, however, which the story poses is: What is the worth of a man who spends the rest of his days alone on a desert island? The Christian answer to the problem, which would also be Dostoevsky's answer, is that the dignity of a man in such straits is in no way diminished, because it is imputed to him by God. It does not *essentially* depend upon his social contribution but upon the immortality of his soul and his capacity to glorify God, even outside a social context. His essential dignity is not owing either to society or to himself.

Given the premises of Communism, on the other hand, the notion that man draws his dignity from God is intolerable because atheism is the first principle of Communism: the authority of the Bible or of the Church must never be allowed to usurp the authority of the State. Furthermore, if Communism were to permit a man to be the arbiter of his own worth, the result would be an intolerable autonomy which would militate against the building of a communist society. Communist theory doesn't quite know what to make of a man who lives all by himself. He has no social value, no civic value, and therefore he has no value at all. It is no wonder that Moldovantsev's editor insisted that Moldovantsev write his story all over again.

It is true that, in the world of the atheist existentialists, a man living on a desert island does indeed have worth if he himself believes in his worth. If indeed it were within a man's compass to find a meaning to life in a godless world, there would be no serious problem, but it is a human phenomenon that men are commonly convinced of their own worthlessness. Furthermore, thinkers who truly think about the meaning of life in a godless world eventually arrive at the conclusion of the most thoughtful existentialist atheists, the conclusion that, as Camus observed, "fundamentally nothing matters," that the life of a man with all his intense and contradictory thoughts and feelings and actions has no meaning, and is in fact absurd. The atheist existentialist denies John Donne's dictum that "No man is an island"; in their view all men are islands and no one else really lives on anyone else's island or ever *can* live on it. Permanent alienation is at the very heart of atheist existentialism. Man is alienated from God because there is no God, and he is alienated from other people because he cannot be other people.

All this in the face of their realization that ultimately men cannot live without meaning in their lives. The words of the Grand Inquisitor ring in the ears of 20th-century man as well as 19th-century man: "Without a stable conception of the object of life, man would not consent to go on living, and would rather destroy himself than remain on earth, though he had bread in abundance." And yet the Grand Inquisitor could not believe any more than the atheist existentialists can believe.

Nietzsche is in some ways the driving force behind the atheist existentialists because he was the first major philosopher to recognize so agonizingly—as agonizingly perhaps as Ivan Karamazov himself—the problem of the meaning of life in a godless world. Nietzsche perceived that "there never was a greater event" than the death of God and that we ourselves "have to become gods to be worthy of it." And so he rose, like Satan from the floor of Hell, to the challenge of becoming a god himself, by constructing a theory of the superman in which God is not only not a lost ally but the chief adversary.

Similarities between Nietzsche's and Dostoevsky's thought have been duly, indeed unduly, emphasized by scholars. Certainly there is a meaningful similarity in their insistence upon man's irrationality and in their consequent distrust of the complacent rationalism of the heirs of the Enlightenment. They agree, too, on the impossibility that science can provide a meaning to human existence; they are both contemptuous of the ideology of progress which infected the 19th century; and they both had a dark presentiment that some awful cataclysm was going to overtake the world.

But such agreements lose much of their significance in the face of Dostoevsky's insistence upon the ultimate authority of God's word and Nietzsche's insistence upon the ultimate authority of man's word. André Gide saw the yawning gap between them when he pointed out that Nietzsche was "jealous of Jesus Christ, jealous to the point of madness," and that he wrote *Zarathustra* and *Anti-Christ* and *Ecce Homo* in conscious competition with the Gospels, whereas Dostoevsky "bowed his head humbly before Jesus Christ."

The atheist existentialists were the anti-spiritual heirs of Neitzsche in that they, too, developed a highly sensitive perception of the problem of the meaning of life in a godless world. Among the atheist existentialists perhaps none have registered with greater sensitivity the problems of living in a godless world than Sartre and Camus, for they were able to express their anguish in the form of plays and novels as well as philosophical essays. Sartre's *Nausea* affords one of the 20th-century's most powerful descriptions of what life should be like to the true unbeliever. "Here we sit," says Roquentin, "all of us, eating and drinking to preserve our precious existence and really there is nothing, nothing, absolutely no reason for existing." *Nausea* is an exquisite portrayal of the ultimate futility of all human actions and aspirations and effort in a godless world. Roquentin experiences the stench of life at every turn.

But for all his unbelief Sartre is a sort of Christian fellow-traveller, a very imperfect unbeliever whose moral values are embarrassingly like Christian values and who had a long way to go before he could attain the perfection of Pyotr Verhovensky's logical atheism. Given Sartre's understanding of what *engagement*, commitment, ought to be, a truly logical atheist could shoot any and all of Sartre's social ideas and ideals full of philosophical holes. So, too, could Dostoevsky.

On balance, it may be that Camus has communicated a greater sensitivity and understanding of the problems attending unbelief even than Sartre, or indeed any other 20th-century writer, greater perhaps than anyone since Dostoevsky himself. His famous opening statement in *The Myth of Sisyphus* that the only really serious philosophical problem is the problem of suicide, suggests something of his understanding. Camus ultimately came out against suicide, though not on any very convincing grounds. "Make known to us the truth about this world—which is that it has none," Caesonia declares in *Caligula*, "and grant us strength to live up to this verity of verities." In fact in *Caligula* Camus, if anything, surpasses Dostoevsky in his ability to portray the truly logical atheist, even Pyotr Verhovensky in *The Possessed*, an adaptation of which he was to write for the stage.

Caligula's aim is to deny all self-denial, to come as close as he can to quenching his thirst for absolute freedom. Furthermore, given the premise of a godless universe, Camus can legitimately present Caligula as having achieved happiness through human slaughter. "I live,

I kill," he says, "I exercise the rapturous power of a destroyer, compared with which the power of a creator is merely child's play. And this, *this* is happiness; this and nothing else—this intolerable release, devastating scorn, blood, hatred all around me, the glories of isolation of a man who all his life long nurses and gloats over the ineffable joy of the unpunished murderer; the ruthless logic that crushes out human lives." Camus in *Caligula* understands quite as well as Dostoevsky in *The Brothers Karamazov* that "if there is no immortality there is no virtue and everything is lawful." Indeed, as Caligula's friend says, Caligula's way is "logical from start to finish."

The Stranger is a starker and more powerful portrayal of human life in a godless world even than *Nausea*, if for no other reason than that it is more artistically compelling, and as such it stands as one of the great 20th-century monuments to the world of unbelief.

And yet for all of Camus's acute perception of the consequences of unbelief he is not able to communicate more than a little understanding of the power of religion, or indeed of the religious mind or the religious argument. This dimness is perhaps most evident in his summary treatment of belief in *The Myth of Sisyphus*, but it shows up too in *The Stranger* and *The Plague*, in which the religious argument becomes almost a mockery. In *The Plague*, for example, Dr. Rieux, the humanitarian unbeliever, discusses the nature of love with the believer, Father Paneloux. Dr. Rieux's arguments in favor of earthly love are delivered with such a superior air that Father Paneloux's weak arguments in favor of heavenly love appear even weaker. Dr. Rieux reiterates Ivan Karamazov's declaration that he cannot accept a scheme of things which permits the torture of innocent children. He is concerned with man's health, he says, not his salvation, and what he hates most is death and disease, i.e., comfort becomes the ultimate aim in life. To such apparently final conclusions, Father Paneloux's sputterings about grace and the need to love what we cannot understand are no match. To his pathetic question, "I haven't convinced you?" Dr. Rieux replies, "What does it matter?" Dr. Rieux is no Ivan Karamazov and Father Paneloux is certainly no Father Zossima, and in presenting both the side of belief and the side of unbelief Camus is no Dostoevsky.

Both Camus and Sartre had talked themselves into some faint hope that man can somehow make it without God after all. The appeal to human fraternity was Camus' ultimate appeal; Dostoevsky, on the other hand, saw that human fraternity without God was not possible. Men will not love other men, he says over and over again, unless they love God first. For all of Camus' and Sartre's sensitivity to the problem of unbelief they could not perceive the truth of Dostoevsky's truth.

Dostoevsky and the Atheist Humanists

Dostoevsky knew that the agony of unbelief may be the first step toward belief, and that the agony of unbelief can come only when unbelievers ask the right questions. Many of the atheist existentialists did ask the right questions even though they gave the wrong answers. But not all the atheist intellectuals in the world today are uncomfortable, nor do they tend to ask the right questions, especially those who are broadly described as atheist humanists. Most atheist humanists are not merely comfortable but cozy in their atheism; that is, they still insist that man can get along without God, much better without God, in fact, and that reason and science in the Enlightenment tradition can lead men to goodness, or happiness, or both. The Marxists constitute the largest group among these because they have enjoyed the greatest political success, if not philosophical success. But the atheist humanist tent is so large that there is plenty of room for anti-Marxists too, who believe that the truths of science and reason should not lead to Communism but to something else.

Just what that "something else" is has been elaborately set forth in two position papers jointly published forty years apart as *Humanist Manifestos I* and *II*. *Humanist Manifesto I* was published in 1933 under the aegis of John Dewey, one of the most influential atheist intellectuals in America. Its signers referred to themselves as "religious humanists," but its intent was to strip religion of all doctrine and to strip God of all power, including even the minimal function of creating the universe. "Religious humanists," it declares, "regard the universe as self-existing and not created." Furthermore, it insists that "the nature of the universe depicted by modern science makes unacceptable any supernatural or cosmic guarantee of human values," thereby repudiating the authority of revelation and the Bible.

With greater candor, *Humanist Manifesto II*, (published in 1973), dropped the epithet "religious" and instead used the term "humanist" without modification. *Humanist Manifesto II* was signed by 114 intellectuals representing a wide range of specialties. The list runs heavily, however, to scientists, social scientists, and philosophers, though it also includes ministers and rabbis, a couple of poets, and the then President of the Illinois Gas Company. The names of some 150 more intellectuals have since been added, and no doubt thousands more names can now be mustered. The anti-religious spirit of the second document is more nearly naked than the first. "Humanists," the Preface explains, "still believe that traditional theism, especially faith in a prayer-hearing God, assumed to love and care for persons, to hear and understand their prayers, and to be able to do something about them, is an unproved and outmoded faith."

In light of a reading of Dostoevsky there is something peculiarly imperceptive, indeed naive, about the statement in the Manifesto that "We find insufficient evidence for belief in the existence of the supernatural; it is either meaningless or irrelevant to the survival and fulfillment of the human race," and indeed it chastizes any humanists who might want to "update" religion rather than, ideally, to destroy it.

Given such premises, *Humanist Manifesto II* comes down hard on such concepts as personal immortality, without which, Dostoevsky concluded, no religion can be viable, and no morality can long endure. "There is no credible evidence that life survives the death of the body," it declares, and "promises of immortal salvation or fear of damnation are both illusory and harmful."

On the other hand, *Humanist Manifesto II* reaffirms its commitment to the positive belief in the "possibilities of human progress" not only by repudiating religion, which it insists impedes progress, but by deifying science and the scientific method, and less crucially, reason and the rational method. "Any account of nature should pass the tests of scientific evidence." "We need," it says, "to extend the uses of scientific method, not renounce them" in order to build "constructive social and moral values."

An optimistic view of a world without God requires an optimistic view of human nature, a more optimistic view, in Dostoevsky's opinion, than the facts will warrant. The section on ethics reflects how good natural man is assumed to be. "Ethics," it declares, "is *autonomous and situational* [italics in text], needing no theology or theological sanctions." It "stems from human interest and need," and is thus predicated upon the belief that man will act in accordance with his own advantage and the advantage of society. It takes no cognizance of what Dostoevsky says is really man's "greatest advantage" in *Notes from the Underground*, the advantage which, Dostoevsky insists, will "cause all systems to crumble into dust on contact," namely the advantage of free will, of whim, of being in charge of one's own soul.

Humanist Manifesto II shows the same blind faith in science and the unaided reason as the 18th-century Enlighteners, whom Dostoevsky perceived to be the Endarkeners. "Reason and intelligence," it declares, "are the most effective instruments that humankind possesses," and "the controlled use of scientific methods . . . must be extended further in the solution of human problems."

To Dmitri's anguished cry, "How is man going to be good without God?" the reply of the *Manifesto* is "by virtue of reason-and-science." Expressed differently, it is the reply of Rakitin in *The Brothers Karamazov*: "Humanity will find in itself the power to live for virtue even without believing in immortality. It will find it in love for freedom, for equality, for fraternity." Dostoevsky was much concerned to demonstrate the untenability of Rakitin's conclusions, as he would have been of the conclusion of *Humanist Manifesto II*, because he saw that ultimately neither freedom nor equality nor fraternity are possible without belief in God-and-immortality.

Despite the acknowledgment in *Humanist Manifesto II* of the dangers and disadvantages of science, and even the limitations of reason, what is striking about it is the total absence of any sense of the dangers or limitations of a world without God. There is none of the spiritual agonizing of Ivan Karamazov; there is only the crude confidence of Rakitin; nor is there anything of the sense of tragedy or loss which Nietzsche experienced as he imagined a world without God, and certainly there is nothing of the acute awareness of the consequences of unbelief of some contemporary atheist existentialists. On the contrary, the premise of *Humanist Manifesto II* is that its laudable goals can be achieved only if religion is abolished.

The *Humanist Manifestos* seem, in their ways, to be not only astonishingly unimaginative, but strangely antiquated. *Humanist Manifesto I* resembles an 18th-century deist document. *Humanist Manifesto II*, although only a few years old, is more nearly like productions of the 19th-century. At this rate, the atheist humanists have perhaps a century to go before they catch up with the atheist existentialists.

There is much to suggest that the spirit of *Humanist Manifesto II* represents the dominant spirit of intellectuals today, particularly in America. In fact, it may be said that in general the problem of the meaning of life in a world without God is more acutely and accurately perceived by European intellectuals than by American intellectuals, that Europe has produced more Ivans, who live in an agony of unbelief, whereas America has produced more Rakitins, with a naive belief that somehow reason and science will see us through. America's relatively short historical experience may have something to do with an excusably unwarranted faith in human nature. Kafka and Camus more nearly represent the European reaction to the idea of a world without God, whereas *Humanist Manifesto II* represents more nearly the spirit of American intellectuals (despite a few European guest signatories). Americans are somehow less willing to admit the defeat of reason and science than West Europeans. The worship of psychological and sociological research, for example, is to an amazing degree an American phenomenon. Kafka and Camus are not perfectly comprehensible—and certainly not acceptable—to the American cast of mind. The same may also be said of the conclusions of Kirkegaard and Dostoevsky.

One might venture that the archetypically American response to the nagging question, "How should one live in a Godless universe?" is given by B. F. Skinner. Skinner, predictably, was one of the signers of *Humanist Manifesto II*, and in some ways he represents the ultimate in psychological know-how, American style.

Whereas *Humanist Manifesto II* is merely a description of certain fundamental atheistic principles based upon the premise of man's natural goodness and offers no social engineering program, Skinner calls for stern measures involving a society made up entirely of the Manipulators and the Manipulated. His proposal suggests embarrassing similarities to the proposal of the Grand Inquisitor, whose concept of a utopia consists of "the hundred thousand who rule over" and "subdue a turbulent flock of thousands of millions." Even the title of his book, *Beyond Freedom and Dignity*, suggests the similarity. Both attempt to force men to be happy, even against their will, in a Godless universe.

Skinner is not very clear about who the Manipulators should be, especially who the Master Manipulator should be, and above all he is not clear as to who should manipulate the Master Manipulator, except that it will not be God. But even if the Master Manipulator were someone like Plato's philosopher-king there is no certainty that he would possess enough wisdom or kingliness to manipulate those who refused to be manipulated, that is, those who stick out their tongues at the Crystal Palace as Dostoevsky's Underground Man does. (If the Crystal Palace becomes too crystallized everyone will be sticking out his tongue at it.)

And yet, given Skinner's atheistic premises, there is a kind of deadly logic to the construction of a Skinnerian world box, for if men are merely super-beasts without souls and free from the threat or promise of personal immortality, then beastly happiness ought to be their *summum bonum*; and since they seem incapable of achieving it on their own, as Dostoevsky has devastatingly demonstrated—indeed seem bent on unhappiness, even destruction and self-destruction—then they ought not to object to letting someone achieve happiness for them. One is almost tempted to say, in fact, that if Dostoevsky is wrong, then B. F. Skinner is right; for as Dostoevsky tried to demonstrate over and over again, if there is no God-and-immortality, then such burdens as freedom and dignity and moral responsibility and suffering and spiritual yearning should all be eliminated in the interest of greater human comfort, and a social scheme that gets rid of them is what men ought to seek.

And yet, just as Christ kissed the agonized Grand Inquisitor after hearing his case for correcting Christ, so also might Dostoevsky have kissed the comfortable B. F. Skinner after hearing his case against freedom and dignity. Christ needed to say nothing further to refute the Grand Inquisitor because He had already refuted him; so too Dostoevsky need say nothing further to refute Skinner. He, too, has also already refuted him.

The point that Dostoevsky always leads back to is that unless men's dignity is in God's hands it is in man's hands, and given the nature of man, it is most precariously in those hands. Society in the West, for example, has now arrived at the stage in which it quarrels over whether foetuses can be destroyed at three months or six months, whether euthanasia can go beyond withdrawal of artificial life support, and whether suicide should be permissible, even encouraged in certain instances. But the only reason that hesitation and controversy over these questions still exist is that the remnants of religion still exist. Without religion, it will be perceived just how logically unassailable is the extermination of the physically and mentally deformed, the sick, the weak, the very young (however far in or out of the mother's womb) the very old, the not so young, the not so old, the black, the white, or, for that matter, the rest. Murder for many reasons and suicide for any reason will come to be seen as wholly justifiable, and political execution can become logical as a matter of course.

Dostoevsky, perhaps more forcefully than any other writer, can help us see the logic, indeed the inevitability, of such developments in a world that is wholly free from the influence of religion. Ivan Karamazov understands the phenomenon well enough in his declaration that "there is nothing in the whole world to make men love their neighbors," that there is "no law of nature that men should love mankind, and that if there had been any law on earth hitherto, it would not be owing to natural law, but simply because men believed in immortality." The whole natural law, Ivan observes, "lies in that faith, and if you were to destroy in mankind the belief in immortality, not only love but every living force maintaining the life of the world would at once be dried up. Moreover, nothing then would be immoral, everything would be lawful, even cannibalism. . . . For every individual, like ourselves, who does not believe in God or immortality, the moral law of nature must immediately be changed into the exact contrary of the former religious law, and egoism, even to crime, must become, not only lawful, but even recognized as the inevitable, the most rational, even honorable outcome of his position."

Miusov, the comfortable atheist *par excellence* in *The Brothers Karamazov*, has neither the perception nor the imagination to recognize how right Ivan is in his estimate of the logical consequences of any society abandoning belief in God-and-immortality. "From this paradox, gentlemen," he tells his audience, with all the smugness and sarcasm he can muster, "you can judge of the rest of our eccentric and paradoxical friend Ivan Fyodorovitch's theories."

Dostoevsky hoped that his readers would at least understand that Ivan was more nearly right in his assertion that civilization cannot long continue without belief in God-and-immortality, and that Miusov and Rakitin—and, as it turns out, most 20th-century intellectuals—are more nearly wrong in thinking that it can.

From the same publisher: